FOCUS ON
Comprehension

Teacher's Resource
for Books 1 and 2

Nelson

Thomas Nelson & Sons Ltd
Nelson House
Mayfield Road
Walton-on-Thames
Surrey KT12 5PL

I(T)P® Thomas Nelson is
an International Thomson Company
I(T)P® is used under licence

Text © Louis Fidge 1999
Illustrations © Thomas Nelson & Sons Ltd 1999

First published by Thomas Nelson & Sons Ltd 1999
ISBN 0-17-420296-2
9 8 7 6 5 4 3 2 1
02 01 00 99

Printed in Croatia by Zrinski Printing and Publishing
House, Cakovec

Cover illustrations: Jill Newton
Illustrations: Janet Simmonett, Kate Sheppard
and Sami Sweeten
Design and typesetting: Susan Clarke
Cover design: Clive Sutherland
Production: Claire Walker
Editorial: Anna Fitzpatrick

Acknowledgements
The author and publishers thank the following for
permission to reproduce copyright materials, as
follows:
Faber & Faber for the extract from *Night Mail* by
W H Auden

Please note: we have tried to trace and contact all
copyright holders before publication, but this has not
always been possible. If notified, we, the publishers,
will be pleased to make any amendments or
arrangements at the first opportunity.

CONTENTS

WHAT IS COMPREHENSION?

The *Concise Oxford Dictionary* defines comprehension as 'the act or capability of understanding, especially writing or speech'. In the context of school, the ability to gain meaning from the printed word is of paramount importance.

A helpful way of looking at comprehension is to treat it as a range of skills. Thomas Barrett, quoted in *Reading Today and Tomorrow*[1], suggests a taxonomy of comprehension skills. This provides a very useful model, and was used as a framework for developing and structuring the *Focus on Comprehension* series

Barrett divides reading comprehension into five major skill levels which move from the easy to the difficult in terms of the demands they place on the reader. The categories he suggests are:

▶ Literal Comprehension
This focuses on ideas and information explicitly stated in the text. The tasks may involve recognition or recall of details, main ideas, sequences, cause and effect, character traits and so on.

▶ Reorganisation
This requires the child to analyse and/or reorganise ideas or information explicitly stated in the text. For example, tasks may involve classifying, outlining or summarising.

▶ Inferential Comprehension
This requires the child to use information and ideas explicitly stated in the text, along with intuition and personal experiences as a basis for making deductions and hypotheses. The child is required to use thinking and imagination that go beyond the printed page.

▶ Evaluation
This requires the reader to evaluate a text, by comparing ideas presented with external criteria (such as other similar sources), or internal criteria (such as by drawing on the reader's own experiences, knowledge or values). Evaluative comprehension deals with qualities of accuracy, acceptability, desirability, worth or probability of occurrence.

▶ Appreciation
This involves the subjective response of the impact of the text on the reader. It requires some sort of emotional response to the content, characters or incidents, author's use of language or imagery.

In summary, categories of Barrett's taxonomy of comprehension skills are as follows:
▶ read the lines (using literal comprehension)
▶ read between the lines (using reorganisation and inference)
▶ read beyond the lines (using evaluative and appreciative comprehension).

Focus on Comprehension used this three-fold classification to develop three categories of differentiated activities, designed to help children develop a wide range of comprehension skills.

[1] T. Barrett, quoted in Theodore Clymer, 'What is reading? Some current concepts', Open University 1968 in *Reading Today and Tomorrow*, University of London Press 1972.

STATUTORY AND NON-STATUTORY GUIDANCE

The teaching of reading is a statutory requirement in the UK. *Focus on Comprehension* has been developed against the backcloth of the statutory requirements of England and Wales, Scotland and Northern Ireland and the objectives of the National Literacy Project.

The National Curriculum for England and Wales

The National Curriculum expects that pupils' reading will be developed through the use of progressively more challenging and demanding tasks.

The General Requirements of the National Curriculum state that in order to develop as effective readers, pupils should be taught to:
▶ read accurately, fluently and with understanding;
▶ understand and respond to the texts they read;
▶ read, analyse and evaluate a wide range of texts, including literature from the English literary heritage and from other cultures and traditions.

Key skills, which are identified as important in the Programme of Study at Key Stage 2, are developed in *Focus on Comprehension*, as follows:
▶ Pupils should be taught to consider in detail the quality and depth of what they read.
▶ They should be encouraged to respond imaginatively to the plot, characters, ideas, vocabulary and organisation of language in literature.
▶ They should be taught to use inference and deduction.
▶ Pupils should be taught to evaluate texts they read, and to refer to relevant passages or episodes to support their opinions.
▶ Pupils should be taught how to find information in books ... by using organisational devices.
▶ They should be given opportunities to read for different purposes, adopting appropriate strategies for the task.
▶ Pupils should be taught to distinguish between fact and opinion ... to consider an argument critically ... to make succinct notes ... to re-present information in different forms ... to note the meaning of newly encountered words ... to use indexes.
▶ Pupils should be introduced to the organisational, structural and presentational features of different types of text, and to some appropriate terms, to enable them to discuss the texts they read, such as 'author', 'setting'.

Scottish 5-14 Guidelines

The Scottish 5-14 Guidelines include the following in their guidance to teachers:
▶ Learning to read accurately and with discrimination becomes increasingly important as pupils move through their education.
▶ The importance of meaning should be stressed at all stages.
▶ Reading should always have a purpose which is clear. Pupils must ... learn to recognise the commoner genres of fiction and non-fiction.
▶ The teacher needs to deploy a widening range of techniques such as sequencing, prediction, cloze procedure, evaluating the text, making deductions, comparing and contrasting different texts.
▶ Reading activities should demand that pupils show an overall grasp of a text, an understanding of specific details and how they contribute to the whole, make inferences, supply supporting evidence, and identify intended audience, purpose and features of style.
▶ Teaching strategies ... will help them to make sense of aspects such as plot, characters and themes.
▶ The teacher can focus on texts:
 – by directing (pupils) into the task,
 – by providing questions which ask for literal, inferential and evaluative responses,
 – by asking them (pupils) to demonstrate understanding,
 – by asking readers to use the text as a model for their own writing.

Northern Ireland Curriculum

Focus on Comprehension follows the guidance to teachers addressed in The Northern Ireland Curriculum as shown below.

Pupils should have opportunities to:
▶ read ... from an increasingly wide selection of books;
▶ discuss their comprehension and interpretation of the texts they have read, justifying their responses logically by inference, deduction and reference to evidence within the text;

Northern Ireland Curriculum continued

- learn that different reading purposes require different reading skills;
- acquire the use of skills necessary to locate information within texts;
- (use resources) making use of organisational devices to locate, select, evaluate and communicate information;
- discuss and consider aspects of stories, for example, characters, places, objects and events, paying attention to what is written and how it is expressed;
- discuss texts, exploring ways in which word meanings can be manipulated;
- reconsider their initial response to texts in the light of insight and information which subsequently emerge in their reading;
- encounter a wide variety of texts;
- respond with sensitivity to what they read, developing the ability to place themselves in someone else's position and extending their capacity for sympathy and empathy;
- speculate on situations read about, predict what may happen or consider what might have happened;
- discuss features of language.

The National Literacy Strategy

As well as taking into account the various UK statutory curriculum requirements, *Focus on Comprehension* has been designed to help schools meet the text level objectives of the National Literacy Strategy. *Focus on Comprehension* follows closely the range of texts and objectives for each year specified by the National Literacy Strategy.

The National Literacy Strategy characterises the literary primary-school pupil as one who is able to:

- read … with confidence, fluency and understanding;
- orchestrate a full range of reading cues … monitor their reading and correct their mistakes;
- have an interest in words and their meanings and a growing vocabulary;
- … understand and be familiar with some of the ways in which narratives are structured through basic literary ideas of setting, character and plot;
- understand and use … a wide range of non-fiction texts;
- have a suitable technical vocabulary through which to understand and discuss their reading;
- be interested in books, read with enjoyment and evaluate and justify their preferences;
- through reading … develop their powers of imagination, inventiveness and critical awareness.

COMPONENTS OF FOCUS ON COMPREHENSION

NLS Level	Course Book	Teacher's Resource Book
1	Starter Book (24 pp)	Book 'A' (152 pp) for Starter and Introductory Books
2	Introductory Book (48 pp)	
3	Book 1 (48 pp)	Book 'B' (104 pp) for Books 1 and 2
4	Book 2 (48 pp)	
5	Book 3 (64 pp)	Book 'C' (104 pp) for Books 3 and 4
6	Book 4 (64 pp)	

Pupils' Books – structure and features

▶ Each book is divided into 22 Teaching Units (single A4 pages of stimulus illustrations in the Starter Book; double-pages in Introductory Book and Pupils' Books 1 and 2; two-, three- and four-page units in Pupils' Books 3 and 4)

▶ Each Teaching Unit is structured in the same way, in the Introductory Book through to Book 4, in order to facilitate planning, provide differentiation, make pages easily accessible to pupils.

▶ Five sections appear in each unit, as follows:

Think ahead
– introduces the stimulus reading passage
– poses open-ended questions for whole-class discussion
– provides a clear purpose for reading the passage.

The stimulus passage
– provides the main text to work on
– provides a wide range of fiction and non-fiction texts
– provides progressively more challenging and demanding extracts
– may be used for 'shared' or 'guided' reading.

Thinking back
– provides activities which encourage 'reading the lines', focusing mainly on literal comprehension
– provides suitable activities for a whole class.

Thinking about it
– provides activities at an intermediate level
– encourages 'reading between the lines', focusing mainly on reorganisation and inferential comprehension
– provides activities appropriate for whole class, group or individual work.

Thinking it through
– provides activities at a third, and higher level of differentiation
– encourages 'reading beyond the lines', focusing on evaluative and appreciative comprehension
– provides activities most appropriate for group and individual work.

Teacher's Book – structure and features

The Teacher's Book:

– defines comprehension

– provides information on the aims, approach, and structure of the course

– sets *Focus on Comprehension* in the context of statutory curriculum guidance

– sets *Focus on Comprehension* in the context of the National Literacy Strategy

– provides practical advice on organising and using *Focus on Comprehension* with special reference to the Literacy Hour

– provides detailed answers to each unit

– provides a comprehensive range of further teaching ideas on how to use each unit for further text level activities (in comprehension and writing composition), sentence level and word level work

– includes an accompanying photocopiable activity for each unit

– provides class and individual record sheets and practical assessment suggestions.

Teacher's Book – Copymasters

▶ Each unit has an accompanying copymaster. These copymasters:
– develop or extend the theme or type of activity in the main unit in the pupils' book
– provide a range of activities which may not be appropriate in a textbook format
– provide extracts for comparison or poems/passages by the same author/poet
– provide playlets or poems for performance.

▶ The copymasters may be used alongside the main unit or independently.

▶ They may be used for whole class, group or individual work.

▶ They may be used for homework assignments.

Note: the Starter Book is structured differently from the other pupils' books. This structuring is explained in Teacher's Book 'A'.

OVERVIEW OF RANGE OF TEXTS

Starter Book

Fiction and poetry
Stories with familiar settings; stories, rhymes and poems with familiar, predictable and repetitive patterns, and structures for our culture and other cultures; traditional stories and rhymes; fairy stories; stories based on fantasy worlds; poems with similar themes; plays.

Non-fiction
Signs; labels; captions; lists; instructions; information books and texts; simple dictionaries.

Introductory Book

Fiction and poetry
Stories and poems with familiar settings; traditional stories; stories and poems from other cultures; stories and poems with predictable and patterned language; poems and stories by significant children's poets and authors; texts with language play

Non-fiction
Instructions; alphabetically ordered texts; explanations; information books including non-chronological reports

Book 1

Fiction and poetry
Stories with familiar settings; plays; myths, legends, fables; traditional stories; adventure and mystery stories; poems based on observation and the senses; shape poems; oral and performance poetry; humorous poems; poetry with language play

Non-fiction
Information books; non-chronological reports; thesaurus/dictionary; instructions; letters

Book 2

Fiction and poetry
Historical texts and poems; plays; imagined works; sci-fi/fantasy; dilemmas and issues; stories and poems from other cultures; classic poetry; modern poetry; range of poetic forms

Non-fiction
Newspaper/magazine reports; instructions; information texts; explanations; persuasive writing; discussion texts

Book 3

Fiction and poetry
Stories by significant children's authors; traditional stories (including traditional stories) and poems from other cultures; plays; concrete poetry; classic poetry; narrative poetry; narrative poetry; choral and performance poetry

Non-fiction
Recounts; observational records and reports; instructional texts; explanations; persuasive writing

Book 4

Fiction and poetry
Classic fiction, poetry and drama; TV/film adaptations; range of genres; range of poetry

Non-fiction
Autobiography/biography; journalistic writing; reports; discussion texts; formal writing; explanations; reference texts

Scope and range of individual books
The range of texts is summarised at the front of each of the pupils' books in the form of a scope and sequence chart. This shows the range of texts covered within the fiction and non-fiction categories.

USING *FOCUS ON COMPREHENSION* IN THE CLASSROOM

Focus on Comprehension and the Literacy Hour

Focus on Comprehension has been designed with the National Literacy Project very much in mind. Because it follows closely the range of texts and objectives for each year specified in the framework document, it has great potential for supporting schools teaching the daily Literacy Hour.

Class work

The National Literacy Strategy defines 'shared' reading as a class activity using a common text, such as a text extract in which the teacher reads to and with the class, modelling and discussing texts. *Focus on Comprehension* provides a range of progressively more challenging and demanding extracts and differentiated comprehension questions.

The extract could be shared with the class and discussed, using some of the activities in the pupils' books for discussion or written comprehension responses. (The 'further teaching opportunities' section in the Teacher's Book provides additional suggestions for comprehension work.)

The use of the passage may be extended further to provide related writing composition activities, and classwork arising from the texts at sentence and word level. The 'Further teaching opportunities' section of each unit's lesson notes provides for this.

Group work

'Guided' reading is when the teacher focuses on independent reading. The framework document suggests that it should be 'a carefully structured group activity, involving time for sustained reading. Pupils should have individual copies of the same text. The texts need to be carefully selected to match the reading levels of the group.' The structure of the *Focus on Comprehension* books make them ideal for this purpose. The differentiated comprehension activities provide 'questions to direct or check up on the reading, points to note, problems to solve', and so on, which meet the text level objectives in the framework. The teacher could introduce the text to the group (to familiarise them with overall context, and to point out key words) as appropriate, use the differentiated activities to assess the development of comprehension and offer support to each pupil as required. The copymasters for each unit provide further opportunities for this too.

Independent work

Irrespective of whether *Focus on Comprehension* is used for shared and/or guided reading, it also offers enormous potential for additional independent work. The framework document suggests that 'independent tasks could cover a wide range of objectives including comprehension work, independent writing, vocabulary extension and dictionary work, practice and investigations in grammar, punctuation and sentence construction, phonic and spelling investigations and practice'. Children may be asked to complete some of the activity sections following each unit or the related copymasters at this time for additional comprehension work. The 'further teaching opportunities' section of each unit's lesson notes provides numerous ideas for capitalising on the extract in each unit at text, sentence and word level for independent work.

Assessment and record-keeping

A systematic use of the *Focus on Comprehension* course will help children prepare for the statutory and non-statutory assessment requirements.

The tightly-structured nature of the reading material and the differentiated range of comprehension activities help make the ongoing assessment of the children's reading and comprehension skills easy to monitor. It may be considered desirable to ask children to complete one of the units each term (and/or one of the accompanying copymasters) on separate sheets of paper, to keep in their individual portfolios as markers and records of progress and achievement.

Recording pupils' progress is an important aspect of classroom management and good educational practice. Two record sheets are provided. The Class Record Sheet (see page 10) enables you to maintain an overview on class progress as a whole, whereas the Individual Record Sheet (on page 11) enables you to monitor individual progress and achievement.

CLASS RECORD SHEET

Book _____   **Class** _____

Name	Units																					
	1	2	3	4	5	6	7	8	9	10	11	12	13	14	15	16	17	18	19	20	21	22

Note: It is suggested that a pupil's progress for each unit is indicated as follows:

/ = attempted;   × = completed satisfactorily

Focus on Comprehension Teacher's Book 'B'   Text © Louis Fidge 1999 Illustrations © Nelson 1999   Published by Thomas Nelson and Sons Ltd

INDIVIDUAL RECORD SHEET

Name _____ **Book** _____ **Class** _____

Unit	Comment	Date
1		
2		
3		
4		
5		
6		
7		
8		
9		
10		
11		
12		
13		
14		
15		
16		
17		
18		
19		
20		
21		
22		

Focus on Comprehension Teacher's Book 'B'   Text © Louis Fidge 1999   Illustrations © Nelson 1999   Published by Thomas Nelson and Sons Ltd

FURTHER TEACHING OPPORTUNITIES

Text level

Reading comprehension

▶ Discuss the presentation of the playscript. Point out the differences between a playscript and continuous prose. Identify the characters and how their dialogue is signalled. Discuss the role of a narrator and how the words spoken by the narrator are printed in the text.

▶ Practise reading the play with different children taking the various roles. Consider what sound effects or other stage directions might have been included, and how and where these could have been written.

Writing composition

▶ Try converting the playscript into the form of a story in prose, paying special attention to the way dialogue is set out.

Sentence level

Grammatical awareness

▶ When reading the play, encourage children to take account of punctuation appropriately. Discuss how the punctuation (such as question marks, punctuation marks) affects the way a part is read.

Sentence construction and punctuation

▶ Find two question marks in the text. Discuss why they are used. Encourage children to make up some questions that they would like to know about Oggy and punctuate them correctly.

▶ Consider occasions when exclamation marks are used. Find an example of an exclamation in the text. Think of, and write, some other similar things the cavemen might have said to Oggy, punctuating them correctly.

Word level

Spelling

▶ Draw attention to the verbs ending in 'ing' in the passage, such as living and sleeping. Write the root verb and the verb with the 'ing' suffix and discuss what changes, if any, have been made. (Many verbs simply add 'ing'. Verbs ending in 'e'

drop the 'e' before adding 'ing'.) Think of other examples. Short words, like 'hit' double the last letter, such as hitting. Look for examples in other texts and ask children to write both forms of the verb – with and without the 'ing'.

Vocabulary extension

▶ Use the sentence 'Their life was hard and tough' for discussing synonyms. Ask children to suggest synonyms for other words in the text. Encourage the use of a dictionary or thesaurus to help.

ANSWERS

Thinking back
1 Oggy lived in a <u>cave</u>.
2 Oggy slept on a <u>rock</u>.
3 When they went hunting the cavemen carried <u>clubs</u>.
4 Oggy liked to plant <u>seeds</u>.

Thinking about it
1 Oggy did not like: the creepy crawlies and bats; the damp and the draughts; sleeping on rocks.
2 Oggy liked painting and planting seeds.
3 The clubs were to protect themselves and to hit animals with.
4 a) hard – soft   b) cold – hot   c) nice – nasty
   d) kind – unkind   e) tough – weak

Thinking it through
1 You can tell it is a play by the way the text is set out.
2 A narrator is the storyteller.
3 Every character's lines begin with their names.
4 (open answer)

⇨ *Copymaster*
Cave Dwellers' Clothes
Children are given some factual information about the development of early clothing in the form of a cloze procedure, and are asked to supply the missing words.

⇨ Cave Dwellers' Clothes

Name _____   *Date* _____

Fill in each gap with a sensible word.

People have nearly always worn _____. Early cave dwellers

made clothes from whatever _____ were available. The first

clothes were probably _____ from bark, leaves or feathers.

When it was _____, people began to wear animal skins

to _____ warm. Before they _____ worn, the animal

_____ were scraped. Holes were _____ in them.

Strips of leather were _____ through the _____ to

keep the _____ of fur together. About forty thousand years

_____ someone discovered the needle. _____ soon

became an important tool in _____ clothes.

Focus on Comprehension Teacher's Book 'B'   Text © Louis Fidge 1999 Illustrations © Nelson 1999   Published by Thomas Nelson and Sons Ltd

FURTHER TEACHING OPPORTUNITIES

Text level

Reading comprehension
► Ask the children to find five facts in the text. Discuss what a fact is. Consider how the text differs from a fiction text. Use the terms 'fiction' and 'non-fiction'.
► Discuss how helpful the labels and diagram are, and how much less useful the text would be if it had no accompanying picture.

Writing composition
► Ask children to select and write 'Five Fascinating Facts About Hot Air Balloons'.

Sentence level

Grammatical awareness
► Experiment by changing some of the verbs with similar verbs and discussing the impact on meaning.

Sentence construction and punctuation
► Note and discuss the way the text is presented (such as through the use of captions or labels) and the reasons for this.
► Convert some of the facts in the text into questions, punctuating them correctly.

Word level

Spelling
► Brainstorm words containing the smaller word 'air' (such as fair, hair). Think of other words with the same phoneme sound but which are spelt differently such as 'are' (care), 'ere' (there), 'ear' (bear).
► Discuss the word 'burn'. Think of other words containing 'ur' for spelling practice. Ask children to suggest words containing the 'ir' and 'er' phoneme too.

Vocabulary extension
► Use a dictionary to look up some of the words in the text that might be unfamiliar such as nylon, wicker, pilot.

ANSWERS

Thinking back
1 False.
2 True.
3 True.
4 False.
5 True.

Thinking about it
1 The basket is for carrying people.
2 The metal bottles of gas are for heating the air inside the balloon.
3 The balloon is filled with hot air so it will float. Hot air is lighter than cold air.
4 The pilot probably checks the wind direction so he or she will know roughly where the balloon will be blown.

Thinking it through
1 The pilot keeps in touch with someone in a car so they can follow and collect the balloon and the passengers when it lands.
2 (open answer)
3 (open answer)

➡️ *Copymaster* **Looking Down**
Children are given an aerial view of a park and have to follow written instructions to draw in several things as and where instructed.

 # Looking Down

Name _____ Date _____

You are looking down from a hot air balloon, floating in the sky.
Draw the following things onto the picture:

- ▶ three ducks on the pond
- ▶ a man fishing in a boat
- ▶ two boys kicking a ball on the grass
- ▶ a lady taking her dog for a walk
- ▶ a car on the road

Focus on Comprehension Teacher's Book 'B'   Text © Louis Fidge 1999   Illustrations © Nelson 1999   Published by Thomas Nelson and Sons Ltd

FURTHER TEACHING OPPORTUNITIES

Text level

Reading comprehension

▶ Discuss the context and setting of the text. Ask children what evidence there is that tells you about it. Relate the text to their own personal experiences of similar situations.

Writing composition

▶ The text could be rewritten in the form of a playscript.

▶ Children could write their own stories of similar situations at home, using the 'comic strip with speech bubble' format.

Sentence level

Grammatical awareness

▶ Be aware of the different characters' tone of voice and expression when reading aloud, paying special attention to the significance of punctuation marks.

Sentence construction and punctuation

▶ Consider the device of speech bubbles for the presentation of dialogue in the text (and note the use of 'think' bubbles for the cat!) The text could easily be converted into prose style, using conventional speech marks and punctuation. This would enable many useful teaching points to be made about what exactly goes inside the speech marks and why.

Word level

Spelling

▶ Use the word 'people' to focus on the 'le' letter pattern at the end of words. Brainstorm and list as many other 'le' words as possible. If appropriate, begin to categorise them into sets according to letter pattern, such as 'andle', 'inkle', 'uzzle'.

Vocabulary extension

▶ Talk about the way in which some of the dialogue from the text would have been said, using common dialogue words such as 'shouted', 'asked', 'replied', 'said'. Collect examples from general reading material.

ANSWERS

Thinking back

1 The boy's name is Chips.
2 He is an untidy boy.
3 His mother is cleaning up the house.
4 Chips has a pet cat.
5 Chips does have a younger brother or sister.
6 Chips calls his grandfather Grandpa.

Thinking about it

1 The picture shows the vacuum cleaner making a lot of noise. It disturbs Chips, who is reading.
2 The dust makes the cat sneeze.
3 The cat is going into the garden for some peace and quiet.
4 She probably calls it rubbish because it is just left lying about on the floor.
5 (open answer)

Thinking it through

1 (open answer)
2 (open answer)
3 (open answer) He probably means that they will just have to put up with the inconvenience until Chips' Mum has finished tidying up.
4 It is possible to tell what the cat is thinking, by reading the 'thinks' bubble coming from it.

⇨ *Copymaster*
How a Vacuum Cleaner Works

Children are given a labelled diagram of a vacuum cleaner. Using the information supplied, they are asked to write an explanation of how a vacuum cleaner works.

How a Vacuum Cleaner Works

Name _____ *Date* _____

6 Clean air is blown out here.

1 The plug is plugged in to the electricity supply.

2 The electric motor turns the fan.

3 The fan sucks in dust and air through the tube.

4 This paper bag collects the dust. When it is full, you take it out and empty it.

5 Air and dust are sucked through this tube.

Write some sentences and explain how a vacuum cleaner works.

_____

_____

_____

Book 1 / Copymaster / Unit 3

Focus on Comprehension Teacher's Book 'B'   Text © Louis Fidge 1999 Illustrations © Nelson 1999   Published by Thomas Nelson and Sons Ltd

FURTHER TEACHING OPPORTUNITIES

Text level

Reading comprehension

▶ Discuss the theme of the poem and ask children to relate their own anecdotal experiences of moving or losing a good friend. Ask them to express their opinion of the poem and explain their views.

▶ Consider the way the poem is structured (such as the way it is set out in three verses, each with eight lines). Note that each pair of lines rhymes.

Writing composition

▶ As a class, brainstorm ideas for a poem written by the girl that moved, seeing the move from her point of view.

Sentence level

Grammatical awareness

▶ Read the second verse and leave out all the verbs. Note what a difference this makes. Discuss the function of verbs in sentences.

▶ Draw attention to the way verbs are expressed in the past tense by using the simple sentence structure: 'Today I pack my case. Yesterday I packed my case.' Use this structure for drawing attention to verbs such as 'stay' and 'pack' which have regular past tenses. (They simply add 'ed'.) Do the same for irregular verbs such as 'sleep', 'go', 'catch'.

Sentence construction and punctuation

▶ This poem is very good for working on the use of commas in lists of words.

Word level

Spelling

▶ Use the word 'pack' for introducing work on prefixes. Note what happens to the meaning when it is prefixed by 'un'. Think of other words with the same prefix. Do the same using prefixes such as 'de', 'dis', 're' and 'pre'.

Vocabulary extension

▶ The poem lends itself to categorisation of words, such as things found in the kitchen, bedroom.

ANSWERS

Thinking back

1 Jane lived <u>across the way</u>.
2 The removal men came <u>after breakfast</u>.
3 The men took the big clock from <u>the hall</u>.
4 Jane's bike was <u>red</u>.

Thinking about it

1 The list could include beds, chairs, red carpet, dishes, plates, Jane's toboggan, dolls, the big clock, carpet, pots and pans, kitchen things, sofa, cupboards, chests, kitchen stools, cooker, fridge, gardening tools, Jane's red bike.
2 (open answer) The writer was Jane's friend. She often played with Jane. The poem talks of the 'sofa where we played'.
3 Yes, the writer did stay at Jane's house. The poem talks of the sofa 'where I slept, the night I stayed'.
4 The last thing the removal men did was shut the front door.

Thinking it through

1 (open answer)
2 (open answer)
3 (open answer)
4 (open answer)

▭▶ *Copymaster* **Open Windows**
The poem is about someone looking through windows, and noticing what is happening in some houses along the street. Children are asked to identify the people and animals mentioned in the poem and label them on the accompanying illustration.

➡ Open Windows

Name _____ Date _____

The windows are open at Number One,
And Dick the canary sings in the sun.

On her piano, little Miss Moore
Practises scales at Number Four.

A kettle is whistling at Number Ten,
Old Mother Moon's making tea again.

At Number Sixteen young Jenny is in;
There's her transistor's happy din!

The window at Number Eighteen is open wide;
You can hear Mrs Chadwick coughing inside.

Tapping his typewriter all the day through,
Mr Gray's working at Twenty Two.

But there's Thirty Three. We hurry on past.
The curtains are drawn and the windows shut fast.

It's dark and unfriendly, cheerless and chill
– And a lean cat sleeps on the window sill.

1 Label the people and animals you can see in some of the houses.

2 Below, write some things you think are happening in some of the other houses:

_____

_____

_____

Book I / Copymaster / Unit 4

Focus on Comprehension Teacher's Book 'B'   Text © Louis Fidge 1999   Illustrations © Nelson 1999   Published by Thomas Nelson and Sons Ltd

FURTHER TEACHING OPPORTUNITIES

Text level

Reading comprehension

▶ Ask children to explain where the passage took place and to provide evidence to support their views.

▶ Look for powerful or descriptive words in the text. Consider why they are used and how effective they are.

Writing composition

▶ Children could use the same idea from the story and write their own about the day 'I took a _____ to school', and how this helped solve some problem or other (such as bullying).

▶ Ask children to write a descriptive passage about the playground and what happens there.

Sentence level

Grammatical awareness

▶ Pick some verbs from the text and ask children to suggest other verbs with a similar meaning, such as: stared – looked; growled – roared; ran – hurried.

Sentence construction and punctuation

▶ When reading the passage, identify and discuss the purpose of the different forms of punctuation discovered.

▶ Note the use of capital letters for emphasis in the word ROARED.

Word level

Spelling

▶ Use the word 'roar' to identify the 'oar' sound. Provide children with the following phonemes: 'or', 'oor', 'aw', 'au', 'ore' and ask them to come up with as many words as possible containing each.

Vocabulary extension

▶ Ask children to suggest as many synonyms as possible for the following common high frequency words: big, little, like, good, nice, nasty.

ANSWERS

Thinking back

1 True.
2 False.
3 True.
4 False.

Thinking about it

Jack Tall came up to the little girl.
The lion told Jack to go away.
The lion started to swish his tail.
The lion roared very loudly.
Jack Tall ran home to his mother.

Thinking it through

1 (open answer)
2 (open answer)
3 (open answer)

➡ *Copymaster*
The Lion and the Mouse

This is a simple retelling of the well-known traditional story. Children are asked to complete sentences based on the story.

The Lion and the Mouse

Name _____   *Date* _____

One day a lion was sleeping in the
shade under a tree. A little mouse ran
over his paw and woke him up. The lion
was not happy at being woken.

'Please don't kill me,' the mouse
squeaked in a frightened voice. 'If you
spare me, one day I will help you.'

The lion roared with laughter. 'What! A little mouse like
you? Whoever heard of such an unlikely thing!' he chuckled.

Some days later the lion got caught in a hunter's net. Try
as he might, he could not free himself. He roared with anger.
Suddenly he heard a tiny squeak. He looked down and saw
the little mouse gnawing at the ropes of the net with her
teeth. She nibbled and chewed until she managed to make a
hole big enough for the lion to escape.

The lion smiled at the little mouse. 'You have saved my life,'
said the King of the Jungle. After this the lion and the mouse
became the best of friends.

Finish each sentence in your own words to retell the story.

One day _____

A little mouse _____

Then _____

Some days later _____

Suddenly _____

The mouse _____

The mouse and the lion _____

Book 1 / Copymaster / Unit 5

Focus on Comprehension Teacher's Book 'B'   Text © Louis Fidge 1999   Illustrations © Nelson 1999   Published by Thomas Nelson and Sons Ltd

FURTHER TEACHING OPPORTUNITIES

Text level

Reading comprehension

▶ Ask children whether the text is fiction or non-fiction and ask them to explain why.

▶ Consider how the way the page is structured helps understanding and locating information such as paragraphs with headings, pictures.

Writing composition

▶ An old-fashioned way for a man to greet a woman, was for the man to raise his hat. Ask the children to write a few sentences and say why they think this might have been the custom. Ask them to give their paragraph a title and to draw a suitable accompanying picture.

Sentence level

Grammatical awareness

▶ Ask children to find a statement, a question and an exclamation in the text. Discuss the difference between each.

Sentence construction and punctuation

▶ Ask children to write some facts they have discovered and to ensure that each sentence begins with a capital letter and ends with a full stop.

Word level

Spelling

▶ Review the various rules for adding 'ing' to verbs. (Many just add 'ing' without changing the root verb – look, looking. Verbs ending in 'e' often drop the 'e' and add 'ing', such as live – living. Some verbs double the last letter, such as spit, spitting.)

Vocabulary extension

▶ Encourage children to use their dictionaries to look up any words in the text they do not know and to write definitions for them.

ANSWERS

Thinking back

1 In some places in <u>Africa</u> people greet each other by spitting in the face.
2 In the Middle Ages <u>kissing</u> was a common greeting.
3 In olden times soldiers used to hold their weapons in their <u>right</u> hands.
4 In <u>Japan</u> people bow to each other when they meet.

Thinking about it

1 It is important to learn how to greet someone correctly otherwise you might upset them.
2 The Dutchman was surprised because he had to kiss every member of the family and the cat as well.
3 The Japanese bow to each other as a mark of respect.

Thinking it through

1 (open answer)
2 The headings and pictures help you find the information quickly.
3 'Bowing' would make a good title for the last paragraph.
4 (open answer)

⇨ Copymaster   Bad Manners

A picture is supplied of people behaving very badly at the dining table. Children are asked to list some of the things that should, and should not, be done when eating.

 **Bad Manners**

Name _____ *Date* _____

The people in this picture are not behaving very well.

List some of the things you should, and should not do, when eating.

Rules for Eating Properly

Focus on Comprehension Teacher's Book 'B' Text © Louis Fidge 1999 Illustrations © Nelson 1999 Published by Thomas Nelson and Sons Ltd

FURTHER TEACHING OPPORTUNITIES

Text level

Reading comprehension

► Discuss the presentation of the two shape poems and discuss how their shape helps to complement each poem.

Writing composition

► Choose single words like pop! shout, snow, fire, tall, mountain and play with them on the board, asking children for their suggestions on how the lettering can be presented in different ways to make a calligram. This could then be extended to phrases or sentences about a snake sliding, (which could be written inside the shape of the thing being described for example).

Sentence level

Grammatical awareness

► Use an awareness of grammar to decipher new or unfamiliar words, such as 'askew', in conjunction with other clues, such as by using the context of the word.

Sentence construction and punctuation

► Note how the letters are different sizes and shapes to help them fit better. Note, too, that there is a mixture of capital letters and lower case letters used in the first poem. Discuss whether this matters or not.

Word level

Spelling

► Find the word 'instead' in the hippopotamus poem. Ask children to supply other words containing the 'ea' phoneme, like 'bread, head'.
► Use the word 'house' to focus on the 'ou' phoneme. Find other 'ou' words and list them. Think of words containing the 'ow' phoneme (as in 'cow').

Vocabulary extension

► Use a dictionary for checking on the meaning of unknown words from the poems.

ANSWERS

Thinking back
1 The first poem is about a <u>house</u>.
2 The roof of the house has a <u>tilt</u>.
3 The wind blows through the <u>walls</u>.
4 The second poem is about a <u>hippopotamus</u>.
5 The hippopotamus just pretends to <u>swim</u>.

Thinking about it
1 'The chimney is all askew' means that the chimney is not straight.
2 The wind probably blows through the walls because there are holes in them.
3 The builder of the house was not very good because the roof has a tilt, the chimney is all askew and the wind blows through the walls.
4 'Amphibious' means something that can move on land and in water.
5 When a hippopotamus is in the water you can only see part of its head.

Thinking it through
1 The poems are presented in the shape of the things they are describing.
2 (open answer)
3 (open answer)
4 (open answer)

➪ *Copymaster* **Shape Poem**
A shape poem in the form of a car is supplied. Children are asked to answer simple questions based on the poem.

➡ Shape Poem

Name _____   Date _____

Boot a-bulging, roof rack rocking,

Dad is driving, Katy's coughing,

Mum has migraine, Granny's grumpy,

Baby's bawling (Gran's lap's lumpy).

Sarah swears and sicks up sweets, Dan the dog is wanting wee-wees.

All around are cars and cases, cones, congestion, furious faces

hauling homeward, slowly, slowly, from a fortnight's (hardly holy!)

"BUMPER B**a**rgain Break-A-Way". We *never left the m***O***torway!*

1 What was:

   a) a-bulging _____   b) rocking _____ ?

2 Who was...

   a) driving _____   b) coughing _____

   c) grumpy _____   d) bawling _____

   e) being sick _____   f) needing the toilet _____ ?

3 List some of the things you think they have got in the boot.

_____

4 Where do you think they were going?

_____

5 Write something you like about the poem.

_____

Book 1 / Copymaster / Unit 7

Focus on Comprehension Teacher's Book 'B'   Text © Louis Fidge 1999   Illustrations © Nelson 1999   Published by Thomas Nelson and Sons Ltd

FURTHER TEACHING OPPORTUNITIES

Text level

Reading comprehension

▶ Consider the use of descriptive words and phrases Lottie uses when she describes what she can see in her imagination. Which words are effective? Why?

▶ Draw attention to the way in which dialogue is presented in the story such as through statements, questions, orders, exclamations. Note, too, how paragraphing is used to organise dialogue.

Writing composition

▶ Ask children to compose a description of an imaginative place, like Lottie's, or of somewhere familiar that they know well.

Sentence level

Grammatical awareness

▶ Consider the function of adjectives; for example, how they describe or add meaning to nouns. Notice how they work in the context of the story.

▶ Experiment with deleting and substituting adjectives in the passage and note the effect on meaning.

▶ Try collecting and classifying adjectives such as for colours, sizes, moods.

Sentence construction and punctuation

▶ Note where commas are used in the passage and discuss their functions in helping the reader.

Word level

Spelling

▶ Use the word 'moonlight' as a way of introducing compound words (words made by joining together two short words such as moonbeam, moonshine). Brainstorm and ask for suggestions of other compound words. Write them on the board as word sums: moon + light = moonlight.

Vocabulary extension

▶ Practise looking up words in a dictionary, encouraging children to learn the quartiles of the dictionary; for example, that 'm' comes around the halfway mark, 't' towards the end.

ANSWERS

Thinking back

1 Lottie had a plaster on her <u>knee</u>.
2 Lottie's mum said she would take the plaster off by <u>magic</u>.
3 Lottie sat down <u>beside</u> her mum on the bed.
4 When Lottie opened her eyes the plaster had <u>gone</u>.

Thinking about it

1 (open answer)
2 When Lottie closed her eyes she could see stars and moonlight, thick snow everywhere and a fairy castle made of crystal glass.
3 She probably snuggled closer to her Mum because her Mum was nice and warm.
4 Lottie was surprised because her plaster had gone and she hadn't felt it being taken off.

Thinking it through

1 Lottie's mum distracted Lottie, by asking her to close her eyes and concentrate on other things.
2 (open answer)
3 (open answer)
4 (open answer)

⇨ Copymaster   Braille

The passage in the unit is about the girl imagining things with her eyes closed. The copymaster provides a Braille Alphabet and asks children to decode a sentence written in Braille symbols.

Braille

Name _____   Date _____

Braille is a method of helping blind people read. It was invented by Louis Braille two hundred years ago. It consists of raised dots on paper which the blind person feels with their fingers and 'reads'. Each letter has a different pattern of dots. Here is the Braille Alphabet:

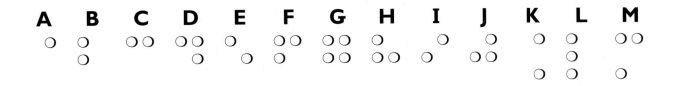

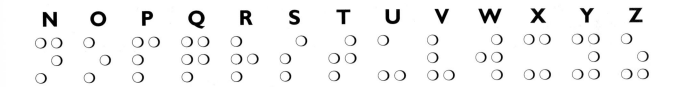

'Read' this Braille message. Write what it says underneath.

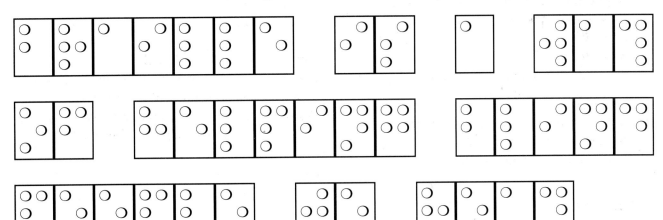

_____

_____

_____

_____

Focus on Comprehension Teacher's Book 'B'   Text © Louis Fidge 1999   Illustrations © Nelson 1999   Published by Thomas Nelson and Sons Ltd

FURTHER TEACHING OPPORTUNITIES

Text level

Reading comprehension

► These two reviews provide an opportunity to discuss the differences between a fiction and non-fiction book.

► The reviews are a mixture of fact and opinion. Discuss which is which, and consider the use of opinion to try to influence or persuade.

► Look at other book covers and discuss their features such as titles, author and publisher names, use of pictures and book blurbs.

Writing composition

► Encourage children to use the reviews as a model for composing a review of their own on a book they have recently read.

Sentence level

Grammatical awareness

► Ask children to identify the adjectives in the reviews. Try reading them without the adjectives and notice what a difference this makes!

Sentence construction and punctuation

► Max the hedgehog gets awfully confused and often gets his words in the wrong order. Provide the children with some sentences in which the words are placed in the wrong order and ask them to rewrite them correctly.

Word level

Spelling

► 'Hedgehog' is a compound word, made from two smaller words. Have fun making up imaginary animals by joining together a random list of nouns and a random list of animals, such as 'lampcat'!

Vocabulary extension

► Try rewriting the blurb on *Focus on Mammals*, but giving it the opposite meaning; for example, 'This fat, hard-to-read, paperback book …'

ANSWERS

Thinking back

1 *The Hodgeheg* is by Dick King-Smith.
2 *The Hodgeheg* is about Max the hedgehog.
3 *Focus on Mammals* is an information book.
4 You can discover why zebras are striped in *Focus on Mammals*.

Thinking about it

1 The books are both about animals.
2 The publisher of *The Hodgeheg* is Antelope. The publisher of *Focus on Mammals* is Gloucester Press.
3 Max is a little mixed up because he was knocked over and bumped his head.
4 This means that the pictures are so vivid they are really life-like.
5 This means that the book is packed full of facts.

Thinking it through

1 (open answer)
2 Printing words in capital letters helps to emphasise a point.
3 (open answer)
4 Some of the facts that could be mentioned are: the book is by Jane Parker; it is published by Gloucester Press; it is a hard-backed book; it contains a lot of facts about animals, including zebras and wolves; it contains photos and drawings.

➩ *Copymaster*   **Book Review**

The copymaster is in the form of a 'book review' template. Children are asked to complete it and write a review of a story book recently read. (The template may be used again and again.)

 # Book Review

Name _____ *Date* _____

Book title _____

Author _____ Publisher _____

Draw your favourite character:

Why do you like this character?

_____

_____

_____

_____

_____

Was there a character you did not like? Why didn't you like this

character? _____

Write two or three sentences and say what the story was about.

_____

_____

What was your favourite part of the story? Say why.

_____

_____

What sort of story was it? Tick the best word or add your own.

adventure ☐   animal ☐   folk tale ☐   historical ☐   ghost ☐

How many marks out of ten would you give the story? ☐

Focus on Comprehension Teacher's Book 'B'   Text © Louis Fidge 1999 Illustrations © Nelson 1999   Published by Thomas Nelson and Sons Ltd

FURTHER TEACHING OPPORTUNITIES

Text level

Reading comprehension

▶ Ask individual, pairs or groups to prepare and rehearse the poem for a performance, identifying appropriate expression, tone and volume, taking note of punctuation and meaning. Discuss the fact that the poem is from the West Indies and consider any unknown words.

Writing composition

▶ Encourage children to find other number poems and to make up their own, on a similar theme or one of their own choosing.

Sentence level

Grammatical awareness

▶ Read the poem again, but this time miss out all the adjectives. Discuss what effect this has.

▶ This poem is good for work on singulars and plurals. Identify the nouns in the poem that have been pluralised. Write both the singular and plural form on the board. Notice what differences occur to the spelling. Note, too, that the word 'fish' can be either singular or plural.

▶ Note that all the words that are pluralised are nouns.

Sentence construction and punctuation

▶ Note the use of capital letters at the start of each line of the poem.

Word level

Spelling

▶ Use the poem as a way of investigating the spelling of plural nouns. Most nouns just add 's' such as shells. Words ending in 'sh', 'ch', 'x' or 's' usually add 'es' such as churches. To make the plural of a word ending in 'f' or 'fe', we usually change the 'f' or 'fe' to 'v' and add 'es'; for example, 'wolf – wolves, wife – wives'. To make the plural if the word ends in consonant + 'y', we change the 'y' to 'i' and add 'es'; for example, 'lady – ladies'. Think of other words for each of these rules and list them.

Vocabulary extension

▶ Find words in the poem beginning with the same letter (such as 'five, flying, fish') and arrange them alphabetically according to their second letter.

ANSWERS

Thinking back

1 There were three <u>humming birds sipping nectar sweet</u>.
2 There were eight <u>sugar apples, just out of reach</u>.
3 There were five <u>flying fish gliding through the air</u>.
4 There was one <u>smiling Grandma in a rocking chair</u>.
5 There were two <u>yellow bows tied on braided hair</u>.

Thinking about it

1 The coconuts were hard, hairy and round.
2 The drums were made of steel.
3 The six ladies were in the market.
4 The shells on the beach were conch shells.
5 If there was too much noise the ten sleepy mongoose would wake up.

Thinking it through

1 The words 'tapping out their beat' tell you that the drums were being played.
2 'Sipping nectar sweet' probably means drinking the sweet liquid from flowers.
3 (open answer) The picture and the things mentioned all give clues that the poem is from the Caribbean.
4 (open answer)

⇨ *Copymaster*
Poems to Practise and Perform

Three poems on a school theme are provided. These may be used to read for fun, to practise reading with expression and for performing, being read aloud in any context.

Name _____   Date _____

Here are some poems about school for you to practise reading.
When you are ready, read them aloud to an audience!

Two Times Table

Twice one are two, violets white and blue.
Twice two are four, sunflowers at the door.
Twice three are six, sweet peas on their sticks.
Twice four are eight, poppies at the gate.
Twice five are ten, pansies bloom again.
Twice six are twelve, pinks for those who delve.
Twice seven are fourteen, flowers of the runner bean.
Twice eight are sixteen, clinging ivy ever green.
Twice nine are eighteen, purple thistles to be seen.
Twice ten are twenty, hollyhocks in plenty.

Teacher, teacher …

Teacher, teacher, don't be dumb,
Give me back my bubble gum.

Teacher, teacher, you're the best
When you wear that old string
    vest.

Teacher, teacher, I declare
Tarzan's lost his underwear.

Teacher, teacher, come here
    quick
Stella Brown's been awfully sick

Teacher, teacher, no more
    school
Let's go down the swimming
    pool.

It's school today

I wake up early, it's school today,
I'll get up early and be on my way.
I wash my face, I brush my hair,
I hang my pyjamas on the chair.

The breakfast table is all set,
I'll eat up quickly and feed the pet.
I wave to Mum and shut the gate,
I have to hurry – it's half past
    eight.

The bus has gone, I'll run to
    school.
I pass the shops and the swimming
    pool.
I reach the gate – it's five to nine.
Goodness me! I'm just in time.

Focus on Comprehension Teacher's Book 'B'   Text © Louis Fidge 1999   Illustrations © Nelson 1999   Published by Thomas Nelson and Sons Ltd

FURTHER TEACHING OPPORTUNITIES

Text level

Reading comprehension

▶ Discuss reasons why people write to each other; for example, to recount, explain, enquire, complain, say 'thank-you'. What sort of a letter is this? Draw attention to the form and layout of this invitation, the way it begins and ends and the degree of formality of the language.

Writing composition

▶ Encourage the children to write a fairly formal reply to the invitation, accepting it.

▶ Ask children to consider what information is needed on an invitation they might send to a friend, inviting them to a party. Design and decorate such an invitation.

Sentence level

Grammatical awareness

▶ There are several adjectives used in the invitation. Identify them. Note how some nouns ('ball', 'glass') may be used as adjectives.

Sentence construction and punctuation

▶ Draw attention to the use of capital letters for people's names and special places, events (proper nouns).

▶ The invitation could be used to discuss the use of the first, second and third person when writing. Usually when we write letters we write in the first person 'I'. This is written in the third person, usually reserved for narratives or recounts.

Word level

Spelling

▶ Introduce the idea of suffixes by studying the word 'eagerly'. Show how it is made from eager + ly. Think of other words (adverbs) that end in 'ly' and identify the root word from which each comes. Extend this to words ending with the suffix 'ful' and 'less'. In passing, note how the addition of the suffix changes the word meaning and, in some cases, the spelling of the root word, such as 'beauty – beautiful'.

Vocabulary extension

▶ Encourage children to make up their own definitions for words (such as palace) and to compare them, discussing ways of improving and refining them.

ANSWERS

Thinking back

1 The invitation was sent by Prince Charming.
2 The invitation was sent to Cinderella.
3 It is an invitation to a Grand Ball.
4 The Grand Ball is to take place in the Royal Palace.
5 It will take place on Saturday October 25th at 10 pm.
6 Cinderella will be collected in the Prince's Golden Coach.

Thinking about it

1 The Ball will take place in the evening at 10 pm.
2 (open answer) People would probably dress up in their finest clothes as it is a very special occasion.
3 (open answer) The Prince is probably sending his own coach to collect Cinderella because he wants to impress her.

Thinking it through

1 (open answer)
2 (open answer) The Prince is keen to see Cinderella because he is sending his coach for her, and it says that he is eagerly awaiting her reply.
3 (open answer) When you admire someone, it usually means you like them a great deal, but you can also admire someone without liking them.
4 (open answer)

⇨ *Copymaster* **Cinderella's Diary**
The copymaster shows Cinderella's pinboard, full of things to be written into the correct space in her diary below.

Cinderella's Diary

Name _____ *Date* _____

Read what Cinderella is doing each day this week.
Write it in her diary.

TOP KNOT
Hairdressing
your hairstyling
appointment is on
Friday 3pm

Fitting for ball
gown - Tuesday
10 am

Thursday
morning -
shopping with Polly for
new shoes.

I'll pick you up for
lunch, Wednesday -
Love, from your fairy
Godmother
x

Sunday
Please come for a
picnic in the park
with me
Love Sally

PRINCE CHARMING'S
BALL
to be held on Saturday
at 10 pm

REMEMBER
Music Club on
Monday

Diary		Diary	
Monday		Friday	
Tuesday		Saturday	
Wednesday		Sunday	
Thursday			

Book 1 / Copymaster / Unit 11

Focus on Comprehension Teacher's Book 'B'   Text © Louis Fidge 1999 Illustrations © Nelson 1999   Published by Thomas Nelson and Sons Ltd

FURTHER TEACHING OPPORTUNITIES

Text level

Reading comprehension

▶ Discuss Anancy's character. What was he like? Evaluate his behaviour. Discuss the fact that Anancy is a spider character commonly found in traditional tales from the Caribbean. In this story, what is the main theme (good over evil, wise over foolish)?

▶ Find and read other Anancy stories and compare them, looking in particular at the character of Anancy himself.

Writing composition

▶ Present the story as a series of simple storyboards.

▶ Make up another Anancy story in a similar way, perhaps considering what would have happened if Anancy had cornered the market in common sense!

▶ Write a description of Anancy.

Sentence level

Grammatical awareness

▶ Anancy had a pot of common sense. Use this as a way of discussing collective nouns. Write a few on the board as starters, such as a tin of beans, a pack of cards, a flock of sheep to give children the idea and ask for other suggestions.

Sentence construction and punctuation

▶ Try retelling the story in the first person as if you were Anancy. Notice the difference this makes. Discuss the fact that stories are usually written in the third person (like the one in the unit).

Word level

Spelling

▶ Look at the word 'climb' from the story. Draw attention to the silent 'b' in it. Think of other words with a silent 'b'. Consider other letters that are often silent in words and group them according to their silent letters, such as silent 'k', silent 'w', silent 'g'.

Vocabulary extension

▶ Explore opposites, such as rude/polite, using words from the story (found, large, began, top, laughing …)

ANSWERS

Thinking back

Anancy wanted to collect all the common sense in the <u>world</u> so he could become the most <u>powerful</u>. He put the common sense in a <u>calabash</u>. He tried to carry the calabash up to the <u>top</u> of a tree to <u>hide</u> it. Anancy <u>dropped</u> the pot and <u>broke</u> it.

Thinking about it

1 Anancy wanted to hide the calabash at the top of the tree so no one could steal it.
2 Anancy had difficulty climbing the tree because the calabash kept getting in his way.
3 Anancy got annoyed because a little boy told him he was silly and gave him some advice.
4 When he got annoyed, Anancy threw the pot to the ground and broke it.

Thinking it through

1 foolish   silly
2 (open answer)
3 (open answer)

⟹ *Copymaster* **The Spider's Web**
Four pictures, which show a spider constructing its web, have to be cut out and sequenced in the correct order. The appropriate caption for each picture then has to be determined.

The Spider's Web

Name _____ *Date* _____

1 Cut out the pictures of the spider making a web.
2 Arrange them in the right order.
3 Stick them in your book.
4 Cut out the sentences and match them to the correct pictures.
5 Stick each sentence under the correct picture.

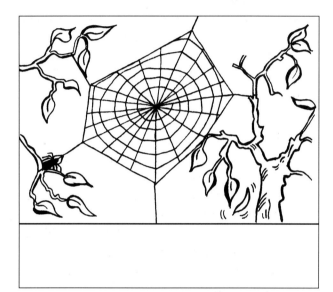

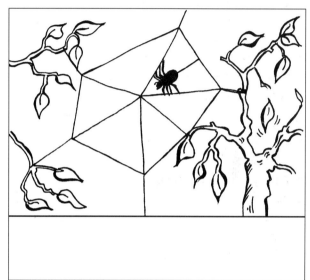

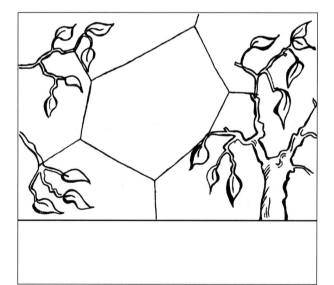

Next the spider makes the spokes of the web.

The spider makes a spiral from the centre of the web.

Last of all, the spider waits to catch his dinner in the web!

First the spider makes the frame of his web.

Focus on Comprehension Teacher's Book 'B'   Text © Louis Fidge 1999 Illustrations © Nelson 1999   Published by Thomas Nelson and Sons Ltd

FURTHER TEACHING OPPORTUNITIES

Text level

Reading comprehension

▶ Ask children what is the purpose of the Country Code. Who is it intended for? Use the words, rules and instructions in the given discussion. Consider other occasions when rules or instructions might be written down, such as plans, recipes, timetables.

▶ Draw attention to the clear, concise sentences (orders or commands) and the way they are set out, using bullet points. Why is this style of layout important?

Writing composition

▶ Encourage the children to write their own instructions, using the poster as a model to help them structure their writing. Begin by writing about something that children have actually made recently, in technology, for example. Broaden this to everyday activities such as 'how to make a telephone call', 'bath a dog'. This can be further extended to rules for playing games, recipes and so on.

Sentence level

Grammatical awareness

▶ Identify the nouns in the poster that have been pluralised. Write both the singular and plural form on the board. Notice what differences to spelling occur. Note, too, that the some words cannot be pluralised, such as litter, wildlife. Can the children think of any more (rain, trousers)?

Sentence construction and punctuation

▶ Discuss the fact that the poster is written in the second person (to you). Although it never actually uses the pronoun 'you' it is implicit.

▶ Try writing each instruction again, in the third person by beginning with either the pronoun 'he' or 'she'; for example, She keeps her dog under control. Notice what changes are necessary.

Word level

Spelling

▶ Use the poster as a way of investigating the spelling of plural nouns. Identify common patterns for pluralising words, for example, we change the 'y' to 'i' and add 'es' (lady – ladies). Think of other words for each of these rules and list them.

Vocabulary extension

▶ Choose ten nouns from the poster and arrange them in alphabetical order.

ANSWERS

Thinking back

1 You should shut all gates behind you.
2 You should keep your dog under control.
3 You should take all your litter home.
4 You should protect all wildlife, plants and trees.
5 You should leave animals, crops and farm machinery alone.

Thinking about it

1 It is important to shut all gates so animals cannot escape.
2 It is important to keep your dog under control so it does not frighten any other animals.
3 It is important not to make a lot of noise so as not to disturb others.
4 It is important to keep to the footpaths so as not to damage farmer's crops.
5 It is important to prevent fires as these can do a lot of damage in the countryside.

Thinking it through

1 (open answer)
2 (open answer)
3 The word 'code' means rules for how to behave.

⇨ *Copymaster*   On My Walk I Saw …
Children have to read and answer clues, associating the correct picture with each clue given. The theme is animals seen in the countryside. The sets of four words then have to be arranged in alphabetical order.

⇨ On My Walk I Saw...

Name _____   Date _____

1 Write the name of each thing in the correct place.

bee   bat   butterfly   bird

This has wings. It has a body like a mouse. It is a _____ .

This has wings. It begins its life as a caterpillar. It is a _____.

This has wings, makes honey and lives in a hive. It is a _____.

This has wings. It has feathers and lays eggs. It is a _____.

2 Now write the four words in alphabetical order.

_____   _____   _____   _____

3 Write the name of each thing in the correct place.

centipede   cow   chicken   cat

This has four legs. It gives us milk. It is a _____ .

This has lots of legs. It is a crawling insect. It is a _____ .

This has two legs. It clucks and lays eggs. It is a _____ .

This has four legs and purrs. It is a _____ .

4 Now write the four words in alphabetical order.

_____   _____   _____   _____

Book 1 / Copymaster / Unit 13

Focus on Comprehension Teacher's Book 'B'   Text © Louis Fidge 1999   Illustrations © Nelson 1999   Published by Thomas Nelson and Sons Ltd

FURTHER TEACHING OPPORTUNITIES

Text level

Reading comprehension

▶ Discuss children's experiences of fairs and theme parks.

▶ Why are plans and maps helpful? Discuss what this particular plan shows and draw attention its special features, such as aerial view, labels and drawings.

Writing composition

▶ Ask children to list all the rides and stall noted on the plan.

▶ Ask children to write directions, explaining how to get from one ride to another.

▶ Children could make a simple plan of the classroom in a similar way.

Sentence level

Grammatical awareness

▶ Use the names of the rides as a way of recognising that pluralisation is one test of a noun, such as Bouncy Castle – Bouncy Castles (only the noun can be pluralised).

Sentence construction and punctuation

▶ Draw attention to the use of capital letters in proper nouns: for example, in the names of the rides and stalls.

Word level

Spelling

▶ Introduce the spelling of comparative adjectives by using some adjectives from the plan as a starting point. Investigate how some words change when -er and -est are added to them, such as 'big – bigger – biggest, bouncy – bouncier – bounciest'.

Vocabulary extension

▶ Give children a list of words taken from the poster, but spelt wrongly (carsel, goast). Ask them to use a dictionary to check the spellings.

ANSWERS

Thinking back

1 Abdi and Shireen were on holiday.
2 They went on holiday in the summer with their parents.
3 The family had a holiday at the seaside.
4 At the seaside there was a fun fair.

Thinking about it

1 When you come in the entrance: a) the Twister and the Ghost Train are on either side of you; b) the Dive Bomber and Big Wheel are straight ahead.
2 The Log Flume is at the centre of the fair.
3 The Bouncy Castle is between the Ghost Train and the Dodgem Cars.
4 The toilets are next to the Café.
5 At the fair you can buy hot dogs and ice creams, and all the things that are sold in the Café.

Thinking it through

1 (open answer)
2 (open answer)
3 (open answer)
4 (open answer)

➡ *Copymaster* **At the Farm**

A plan of a farm is supplied. Children are asked to follow the path around the farm and to list the animals encountered in order and to say whether they are on the left or the right.

⇨ At the Farm

Follow the path around the farm.
Fill in the chart with what you see.

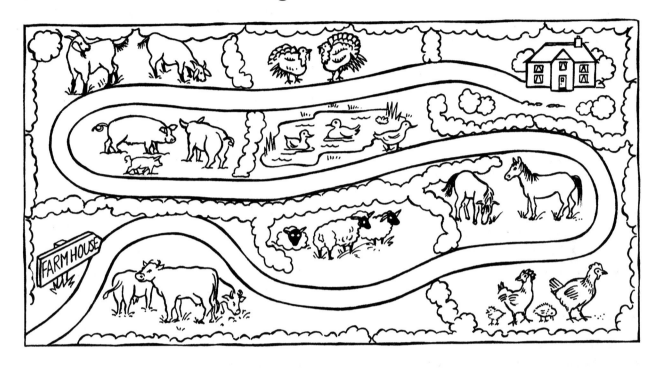

	(Write the name) Things I see on the farm	(Tick the box) on my right	on my left
First	cows	✓	
Second			
Third			
Fourth			
Fifth			
Sixth			
Seventh			
Eighth			

Book 1 / Copymaster / Unit 14

Focus on Comprehension Teacher's Book 'B'   Text © Louis Fidge 1999 Illustrations © Nelson 1999   Published by Thomas Nelson and Sons Ltd

FURTHER TEACHING OPPORTUNITIES

Text level

Reading comprehension

▶ Explain to children that Aesop's Fables are stories with a moral (or a lesson to learn). Discuss what lesson can be learnt from this fable.

▶ Find and read other fables or parables and discuss their meanings.

Writing composition

▶ As a class, write a story plan for the fable. Change the character and setting and then write a story from the plan.

▶ Ask children to make up their own fables, after reading several well-known ones.

Sentence level

Grammatical awareness

▶ Use the fable as a way of introducing the idea of pronouns. Replace all the pronouns in the passage with the noun they stand for, to show their function.

Sentence construction and punctuation

▶ Identify the use of conjunctions in the text, joining two sentences together. Try writing these complex sentences as two or three shorter sentences to demonstrate the function of conjunctions; for example, 'He came to a stream and began to cross over a narrow plank which led from one bank to another.' 'He came to a stream. He began to cross over a narrow plank. The narrow plank led from one bank to another.'

Word level

Spelling

▶ Draw attention to the contraction 'I'll'. Show how the apostrophe stands for a letter or letters ('w', 'i') that are left out. Look for other examples of contractions in reading books. List them and write the longer and contracted form of each.

Vocabulary extension

▶ Find the words 'piece' and 'peace' in the text. Ask the children to write sentences including the words to show they understand the difference. Provide the children with other pairs of homonyms and ask the children to do the same with them, such as 'there, their; meat, meet'.

ANSWERS

Thinking back

1 In his mouth the dog was carrying a piece of meat.
2 The dog came to a stream.
3 The dog walked across a plank.
4 In the water the dog saw his reflection.
5 The dog dropped the meat in the water.

Thinking about it

1 The dog was proud of himself because he had found a large piece of meat.
2 He was carrying the meat away so he could eat it in peace.
3 The dog stopped when he saw his reflection in the water.
4 The dog thought he was looking at another dog with a larger piece of meat in his mouth.
5 The dog let go of his own piece of meat when he tried to grab the meat in the reflection.

Thinking it through

1 (open answer)
2 (open answer)
3 Possible answers are:
   a) Do not try to be too clever.
   b) Be happy with what you have got.

⇨ *Copymaster* **The Greedy Man**
The theme of the Aesop's fable in the unit is greediness. This short traditional story is on a similar theme. Children are asked a range of questions based on the story.

➡ The Greedy Man

Name _____   Date _____

A poor man worked for a rich farmer. He was always
complaining. One day the king got to hear about it. The
king asked him what the problem was.

'I do not get paid enough,' he moaned.

The king looked at the man for a while and then spoke.
'Are you honest?' he asked.

'Yes, I am,' replied the man.

'Then one day you will be rich,' said
the king. He gave the man two sacks and
said, 'Take these. The small one is for
you. The big one is for the farmer.'

As the poor man walked home he
began to wonder why the king had only
given him the small sack. Just before he
arrived back at the farm he stuffed the
big sack under a bush.

He gave the small sack to the farmer and told him it was
a present from the king. When he opened it, the farmer was
even more surprised, for it was full of gold coins.

The poor man raced back to the big sack. He was very
excited as he opened it, thinking of all the gold it contained.
But when he opened the sack, it was full of ... seed!

MORAL: Honesty is the best policy.

Who are the three main characters?

_____   _____   _____

Who is the poorest? _____   Who is the richest? _____

Who complained? _____   Who listened? _____

Who was wise? _____   Who was foolish? _____

Who was surprised? _____   Who was shocked? _____

Who was dishonest? _____

Focus on Comprehension Teacher's Book 'B'   Text © Louis Fidge 1999   Illustrations © Nelson 1999   Published by Thomas Nelson and Sons Ltd

FURTHER TEACHING OPPORTUNITIES

Text level

Reading comprehension

▶ Enjoy reading this poem together as a class, concentrating on the rhythm and humour. Discuss which of the verses are nonsense verses and which verse could actually have happened. Notice how the rhyming element of the poem helps prediction.

▶ Ask children to express their views on the poem and make explicit what they liked or disliked about it.

Writing composition

▶ Discuss the repetitive structure of the poem with the class and use it to help make up further verses.

Sentence level

Grammatical awareness

▶ Draw attention to the fact that the poem is written in the first person (as shown by the use of the pronoun I). What happens if the pronoun I is changed to he, she, you, they? (Ensure agreement between subject and verb of the sentences.)

▶ Identify other pronouns used in the poem and who or what each pronoun stands for.

Sentence construction and punctuation

▶ Note, and discuss, the various uses of commas in the poem.

Word level

Spelling

▶ Ask children to look for smaller words hidden within longer words in the poem, such as lion, park, bread.

Vocabulary extension

▶ Discuss what the child might have said when the father gave the child the surprise; for example, 'Wow! What a lovely surprise!' Collect, investigate and classify common expressions from reading and own experience (ways of expressing surprise, apology, greeting, warning, thanking, refusing).

ANSWERS

Thinking back

1 The lion was in the park.
2 The camel was in the rain.
3 The monkey was in the street.
4 The father was in the shop.
5 The surprise was a puppy with big, brown eyes and a little curly tail.

Thinking about it

1 The lion had bread and jam for tea.
2 The camel got wet because it was in the rain.
3 It was a mother monkey because it says she had a baby.
4 It was lunch-time when the monkeys went to Timbuctoo.
5 The puppy's eyes were brown.
6 The puppy had a little curly tail.

Thinking it through

1 (open answer)
2 The father was probably in a pet shop because he bought a puppy there.
3 (open answer)

➡ *Copymaster*
Some Surprising Animals

The 'silly' theme of the poem in the unit is picked up here. Children are asked to join the beginning and endings of silly rhyming sentences and then to make up some of their own.

⇨ Some Surprising Animals

Name _____   Date _____

Join up the beginnings and endings of these rhyming sentences.

I met a bear   with a charming smile.

I met a mole   with holes in his socks.

I met a crocodile   with purple hair.

I met an ape   in the middle of the road.

I met a fox   stuck down a hole.

I met a goat   pushing a pram.

I met a toad   wearing a cape.

I met a lamb   rowing a boat.

Think of a good way of finishing these:

I met a bee _____

I met a calf _____

I met a mouse _____

I met a shark _____

I met a deer _____

I met a slug _____

I met a whale _____

I met a crow _____

Focus on Comprehension Teacher's Book 'B'   Text © Louis Fidge 1999 Illustrations © Nelson 1999   Published by Thomas Nelson and Sons Ltd

FURTHER TEACHING OPPORTUNITIES

Text level

Reading comprehension

► Ask children to retell the main events in the passage in their own words.

► Consider how the children would have felt, learning how to fly.

► Ask the children to comment on the behaviour of the children, such as going off with Peter Pan, not knowing where they were going, not telling their parents. Discuss the wisdom or foolishness of their actions and why they might have done it.

► Consider the credibility of the events described in the story.

Writing composition

► Brainstorm ideas on how the story might develop and plan a more extended story based on the passage as a starting point.

► Try writing the passage again from the point of view of one of the children, as a first person account.

Sentence level

Grammatical awareness

► Michael, the youngest, shouted 'I flewed!' Give children some irregular verbs and ask them to write the verbs in the past tense, such as:
I see – I saw; He catches – he caught.

Sentence construction and punctuation

► Use the text as an opportunity to discuss punctuation conventions related to direct speech and the use of speech marks.

Word level

Spelling

► Use the word 'wriggle' from the text to focus on silent letters. Use a dictionary to find as many other words as possible containing a silent 'w' at the beginning. Consider other letters that are often silent in words and group them according to their silent letters (such as silent 'k', silent 'b', silent 'g').

Vocabulary extension

► Begin with the dialogue words in the unit; for example, called, cried, said, shouted. Look in other texts and collect as many different dialogue words as possible. Draw up a class list and encourage children to use a variety of them in their writing.

ANSWERS

Thinking back

1 Peter had some <u>magic dust</u>.
2 Peter showed the children how to <u>fly</u>.
3 John was wearing his <u>top hat</u>.
4 Wendy was flying near the <u>bathroom</u>.
5 Mr and Mrs Darling arrived just <u>too late</u>.

Thinking about it

Peter blew magic dust over the children.
The children took off from their beds.
Mr and Mrs Darling rushed up the stairs.
The children flew out of the nursery window.

Thinking it through

1 (open answer)
2 (open answer)
3 (open answer)
4 Mr and Mrs Darling knew something strange was happening because they could see four shadows flying around in the children's bedroom.
5 (open answer)

➡️ *Copymaster* **Daedelus and Icarus**

The story of the Greek legend is retold simply in the form of a cloze procedure. Children are asked to supply the missing words.

➡ Daedelus and Icarus

Name _____   Date _____

**Read this Greek story about Daedelus and Icarus.
Fill in each gap with a sensible word.**

Daedelus and his son _____ were in prison on the island of

Crete. One _____ Daedelus thought of a good _____

for escaping. He decided to _____ some wings so they could

_____ away. They made some wings by collecting birds'

_____. They stuck the feathers _____ with wax. When

they had _____ they strapped on the _____ and

jumped _____ a high cliff. Soon _____ were flying

_____ in the sky. Icarus flew higher and _____ and got

nearer and _____ the sun. Suddenly the wax on _____

wings started to _____. He fell into the _____ and was

drowned. _____ was very sad.

Focus on Comprehension Teacher's Book 'B'   Text © Louis Fidge 1999 Illustrations © Nelson 1999   Published by Thomas Nelson and Sons Ltd

FURTHER TEACHING OPPORTUNITIES

Text level

Reading comprehension

▶ Discuss reasons why people write to each other; for example, to recount, explain, enquire, complain, say 'thank-you. What sort of a letter is this? Draw attention to the form and layout of this letter, the way it begins and ends and the degree of informality of the language. (Compare it with the more formal style of the invitation in Unit 11.)

Writing composition

▶ Encourage the children to write letters, notes and messages, to communicate within school. Write letters to authors about books, selecting style and vocabulary appropriate to the intended reader.

Sentence level

Grammatical awareness

▶ Notice the predominance of the first person pronoun (I, me, my). Discuss and distinguish between the first, second and third person personal pronouns (I, you, he, she, it, we, you, they). Discuss whether each is singular or plural (NB 'you' can be either), and whether each is masculine or feminine. Discuss possessive pronouns too (my, your, his, her, its, our, your, their).

Sentence construction and punctuation

▶ Try changing the pronoun in some of the sentences from 'I' to 'she' in the letter and note what changes are necessary to the verbs.

Word level

Spelling

▶ There are several compound words in the letter, such as penfriend. Find and list these, noting how they are constructed. Ask children to suggest other common compound words.

Vocabulary extension

▶ Investigate words which are spelt the same but have two meanings, such as soaps, wave, bank.

ANSWERS

Thinking back

1 Shirleen wrote the letter.
2 The letter was to Amy.
3 Shirleen lives at 14 Downs Road, Luton.
4 Amy lives in a different town.
5 Shirleen has not written to Amy before.

Thinking about it

Some facts about Shirleen:

Shirleen is a girl. She lives in Luton. Shirleen is nearly eight years old. She has black hair. Her Mum calls her 'Sweety' because Shirleen means sweet. Shirleen likes skating and watching soaps on TV. She loves horses. She would love a horse of her own. Shirleen likes music and drawing. Her younger brother is called Ali. Shirleen's house has a nice garden with lots of flowers.

Thinking it through

1 (open answer)
2 (open answer)
3 (open answer)

⇨ *Copymaster*   **The Reply**

The copymaster provides some factual information about Amy. Children are asked to compose a reply to Shirleen's letter (in Unit 18) based on the information supplied.

 # The Reply

Name _____ *Date* _____

Here are some facts about Shirleen's pen friend, Amy. Use them to help you make up a letter, in reply to Shirleen's (in Unit 18).

Personal information
8 years old. Tall. Fair hair. Glasses.

Family information
Older brother Peter. Baby sister Emma. Barker, the pet dog.
Mum keen on gardening. Dad works in car factory.

Favourite things
Likes music and reading. Enjoys walking dog. Likes shopping for
new clothes.

---

12 King Street
Barchester.
September 25th 1998

Dear Shirleen

Love from
Amy

FURTHER TEACHING OPPORTUNITIES

Text level

Reading comprehension

▶ Discuss, prepare and read this poem aloud, making the most of the rhyme, rhythm, sound effects and alliteration in it.

▶ Discuss the structure of the poem, such as verses, each with five lines and chorus. Investigate the method of rhyming.

▶ Invite children to comment on the poem, expressing their opinions and justifying them.

▶ Find, read and compare other nonsense poems and word poems containing language play.

Writing composition

▶ Encourage children to make up a name for an imaginary land and use what they have learned from Spike Milligan's poem, to have a go at writing one themselves, perhaps as a class poem. Encourage the use of alliteration, onomatopoeia and rhythm.

Sentence level

Grammatical awareness

▶ There are some interesting, if somewhat unorthodox, plurals in the poem. Find and discuss these. Revise work on rules governing turning singular nouns into plurals.

Sentence construction and punctuation

▶ Draw attention to the various uses of capital letters and commas in the poem, and the number of times exclamation marks are used.

Word level

Spelling

▶ Discuss the fact that this is a nonsense poem ('non' meaning no). Use a dictionary and look up other words beginning with the prefix 'non'. Do the same with prefixes 'mis' (as in mislead), and 'ex' (as in export), and understand how these prefixes can give clues to the meanings of the words generated.

Vocabulary extension

▶ If possible, use a dictionary which provides further information about words and their origins, to find out what words really mean and where they come from. (For example, 'dandelion' literally means 'the teeth of the lion' from the French.)

ANSWERS

Thinking back

In the Land of the Bumbley Boo, the people are red, <u>white</u> and blue. At the <u>zoo</u> you can buy lemon pie. The people give away <u>foxes</u> in little <u>pink</u> boxes. You will see <u>thousands</u> of cats there. The cats wear trousers and <u>hats</u>.

Thinking about it

1 The people never blow noses, or ever wear closes.
2 You might find a bottle of dandelion stew.
3 A gnu is a kind of animal.
4 The cats' trousers and hats are made of pumpkin and pelican glue.
5 You can get to Bumbley Boo by train.

Thinking it through

1 (open answer)
2 (open answer)
3 a) noses – closes   b) foxes – boxes
   c) cats – hats   d) run – one
   e) The words that rhyme with Boo are: blue, do, zoo, stew, gnu, glue, you.
4 (open answer)

⇨ Copymaster
Some Nonsense Poems to Enjoy

A number of nonsense poems are included on the copymaster to read for pleasure, to practise and to read aloud.

Some Nonsense Poems to Enjoy

Name _____ Date _____

Have fun learning and performing these nonsense poems.

As I was going

As I was going up the stair
I met a man who wasn't there.
He wasn't there again today,
I wish that man would go away!

Imagine...

Imagine if the sea was in the sky,
And trees grew underground,
If all the fish had giant teeth,
And all the cows were round;
If birds flew backwards all the time,
And eagles ruled the land;
If bricks poured down instead of rain,
If all the seas were sand;
If everyone had seven heads
And we all spoke in Double Dutch,
And if the sun came out at night,
We wouldn't like it much.

'Twas midnight

'Twas midnight on the ocean,
Not a motor car in sight,
The sun was shining brightly,
For it rained all day that night.
'Twas a summer's day in winter
And snow was falling fast
As a barefoot girl with shoes on
Stood sitting in the grass.

As I was going out

As I was going out one day
My head fell off and rolled away.
But when I saw that it was gone,
I picked it up and put it on.

And when I got into the street
A fellow cried, 'Look at your feet!'
I looked at them and sadly said:
'I've left them both asleep in bed!'

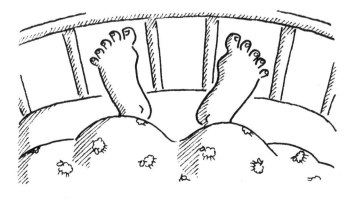

Focus on Comprehension Teacher's Book 'B'   Text © Louis Fidge 1999   Illustrations © Nelson 1999   Published by Thomas Nelson and Sons Ltd

FURTHER TEACHING OPPORTUNITIES

Text level

Reading comprehension
- Refer to any significant aspects of the text, such as opening, build-up, atmosphere, and discuss how language is used to create the words (such as adjectives, adverbs, verbs).
- Discuss Lilly's feelings at certain points, and her behaviour. Ask children to comment on what they think her relationship with her Gran was like.

Writing composition
- Imagine one of the whales carried Lilly away to a secret land. What adventures would she have? What would happen? Brainstorm ideas, and discuss the sort of things that could be written, focussing on language to create effects. Help children plan more extended stories, encouraging the use of paragraphs.

Sentence level

Grammatical awareness
- Ask the children to consider the story from Lilly's point of view in the first person singular. Go through the passage one sentence at a time and consider how it would be written and what changes would be necessary to ensure pronoun/verb agreement.

Sentence construction and punctuation
- Read the sentence: 'There, enormous in the ocean, were the whales.' Pay attention to the commas and the way they are used to mark off the phrase in the middle. Try to make up, and punctuate other sentences, using this as a model.

Word level

Spelling
- Revise syllabification. Choose a selection of two and three syllable words from the text. Say them aloud and ask children to tap the beats of the syllables and say how many each word contains. Practise writing some of the words, marking the syllable boundaries.

Vocabulary extension
- Select some words from the text , such as 'bright' and ask children to suggest synonyms for them. Use a thesaurus to check and extend ideas.

ANSWERS

Thinking back
1 Lilly's Grandmother told Lilly stories about whales.
2 The whales sang and called her name.
3 Lilly dropped a yellow flower on the water.
4 When Lilly woke up she went down to the shore.
5 In the ocean Lilly saw some whales.

Thinking about it
1 (open answer)
2 She dropped the flower on the water as a present to the whales.
3 (open answer) It was possibly the sound of the whales singing and calling out her name.
4 You can tell Lilly ran quickly because it says her heart was pounding as she reached the sea.

Thinking it through
1 a) jetty – a wooden platform which stretches into the sea
   b) ocean – a large stretch of water
   c) spray – drops of water which splash up
2 (open answer)
3 (open answers)
4 (open answer)

⇨ *Copymaster* Under the Sea
Children are provided with a number of clues and pictures relating to things found under the sea. They are asked to draw the missing pictures and to supply the missing name for each thing. Dictionaries may be useful for this.

⇨➧ Under the Sea

Name _____ Date _____

Read the clues. Draw any missing pictures and fill in any missing words. Use a dictionary to help if necessary.

A heavy metal hook used to stop a ship moving. an_____	A shellfish with eight legs and two pincers. cr_____	 d_____
A fish like a snake. e_____	A creature with eight legs called tentacles. o_____	A round, flat shellfish, which sometimes contains pearls. oy_____
  s_____	A boat that can go underwater. s_____	Like a seal with tusks. wa_____

Focus on Comprehension Teacher's Book 'B'   Text © Louis Fidge 1999 Illustrations © Nelson 1999   Published by Thomas Nelson and Sons Ltd

FURTHER TEACHING OPPORTUNITIES

Text level

Reading comprehension

▶ Ask children (in pairs or groups) to prepare and practise reading the poem with due attention to punctuation, expression and meaning, with a view to reading it aloud to the class.

▶ Discuss the language of the poem and ask children to suggest the meaning of words they do not know, such as 'tarried', by using whatever clues are available.

▶ Ask children to suggest a reason why the poet repeats certain phrases.

▶ Find, read and compare other poems by Edward Lear.

Writing composition

▶ Ask children to try and make up their own version of the last verse. Having done that, they can then do the copymaster.

Sentence level

Grammatical awareness

▶ Identify all the verbs in the poem. Ask the children to suggest alternatives and discuss what difference this makes to the meaning.

Sentence construction and punctuation

▶ Read the poem again, and identify all the punctuation marks. Discuss what these signal to the reader, and what their functions are.

Word level

Spelling

▶ Pick selected words from the poem, and identify significant phonemes in them or letter patterns, such as p*ou*nd, eleg*ant*, s*ai*led. Have a timed competition to see who can come up with the most words containing that letter pattern.

Vocabulary extension

▶ Ask children the difference between the homonyms 'fowl' and 'foul'. Investigate other words that sound the same but are spelt differently, such as wood, would.

ANSWERS

Thinking back
1 False.
2 True.
3 False.
4 True.
5 True.

Thinking about it
1 (open answer) The Owl sang a love song to Pussy-Cat.
2 Pussy-Cat said they should get married.
3 In the wood there were Bong-trees.
4 Piggy-wig had a ring at the end of his nose.

Thinking it through
1 Owl really sang to Pussy-Cat, playing the guitar as he sang.
2 (open answer)
3 (open answer)
4 The poem is divided into three verses (although the entire poem is not shown in the unit).
5 The three characters mentioned in the first two verses are Owl, Pussy-Cat and Piggy-wig. The fourth character is Turkey.

➡ *Copymaster*
The Owl and the Pussy-Cat
The children are asked to cut out and resequence the lines of the last verse of the poem, which is not given in the unit. It would be helpful for children to have access to the unit to compare the structure of the verses when undertaking this activity.

⇨ The Owl and the Pussy-Cat

Name _____   Date _____

**Here is the last verse of the poem by Edward Lear –
but the lines are all mixed up!
Cut them out and put them in the right order.**

So they took it away, and were married next day

The moon,

'Dear Pig, are you willing to sell for one shilling

They dined on mince, and slices of quince,

They danced by the light of the moon.

The moon,

Which they ate with a runcible spoon;

Your ring?' Said the Piggy, 'I will.'

And hand in hand, on the edge of the sand,

They danced by the light of the moon,

By the Turkey who lives on the hill.

Focus on Comprehension Teacher's Book 'B'   Text © Louis Fidge 1999 Illustrations © Nelson 1999   Published by Thomas Nelson and Sons Ltd

FURTHER TEACHING OPPORTUNITIES

Text level

Reading comprehension

▶ Discuss the fact that this is a traditional story about how the earth was formed. (Find, read, compare and contrast other such creation stories, if possible.) What words or phrases in it suggest that it is from another culture?

▶ Identify and discuss structure words throughout the story that help sequence the events, such as 'in the beginning'.

▶ Ask children to comment on the behaviour of the different characters in the story. (Were they good, bad, wise, foolish?)

Writing composition

▶ Ask the children to make up their own version of a creation story. Ask for the children's suggestions and ideas and help make a class plan for a story. Encourage the children to use the sort of structural language found in the unit.

Sentence level

Grammatical awareness

▶ Use the passage to help review parts of speech (such as nouns, adjectives, verbs, pronouns). Select one part of speech at a time and go through the passage trying to identify such words, noting the functions they play.

Sentence construction and punctuation

▶ Experiment by deleting, or leaving out words, in the passage as it is read, to discover which are essential to retain meaning and which are not.

Word level

Spelling

▶ Ask children to select ten difficult words from the passage (excluding names). Write them on the board and ask for suggestions on how best to remember their spellings; for example, looking for small words in the middle, known letter patterns, syllabification.

Vocabulary extension

▶ Ask children to suggest definitions for some of the less familiar words in the passage. Use dictionaries to check the meanings of them.

ANSWERS

Thinking back

1 Olorun and the gods swung down to earth on spiders' webs.
2 Orisha Nla did not do as he was told.
3 It was Oduduwa who made the dry land.

Thinking about it

1 Olorun decided to make some dry land because there was only water and marshes.
2 (open answer) Oduduwa probably did the job Orisha Nla was supposed to do because he saw that his brother had gone to sleep and had not done as Olorun had told him.
3 Olorun had to send the Thunder God to keep the peace because Orisha Nla and Oduduwa kept arguing about who the earth belonged to.

Thinking it through

1 (open answer)
2 (open answer)
3 (open answer)
4 (open answer)

⇨▶ *Copymaster*
A Chinese Creation Story

A Chinese version of a creation story is supplied. It is suggested that this is used for reading and discussing, comparing it to the creation story in Unit 22.

Name _____   Date _____

Read this story and compare it with Unit 22 in the pupils' book.

In the beginning there was nothing but mist. Suddenly into this mist came a great light. The mist shook and separated. That which was light rose upwards to form heaven. That which was heavy sank and formed the earth.

Then came two strong forces called Yin and Yang. Yang was like a dragon, hot, fiery and full of energy. Yin was like a cloud, moist and cool, drifting slowly. Together they balanced each other, and kept the world in harmony.

Yang created the sun, Yin the moon. They created the four seasons and water, earth, metal, fire and wood.

The earth was just a ball, without any features so Yin and Yang created the giant P'an Ku. He dug the valleys, piled up the mountains and made the plains until the earth as we know it took shape. He worked so hard that one day he collapsed and died. His huge body became the five holy mountains. His flesh became the soil, his bones the rocks, his hair the plants and his blood the rivers. From his sweat came the rain and from the fleas on his body came the human beings.

What do both stories have in common? _____

_____

Why are they called creation stories? _____

_____

Which did you like best? Why? _____

_____

FURTHER TEACHING OPPORTUNITIES

Text level

Reading comprehension

▶ Set the context of the passage by explaining about the opening up of the American West by settlers, and discuss with the class their reasons for going, the challenges facing them, the hardships they faced, the opportunities and adventures. Ask children to use their imagination and, building on the information in the text, flesh out the setting and the characters. What would they see, hear, smell, experience? What would the house be like? How would they feel?

Writing composition

▶ Encourage the children to empathise with the children in the passage. Extend the discussion above into writing. Imagine some of the adventures the family had. Imagine what will happen next. Ask the children to write it in the first person.

Sentence level

Grammatical awareness

▶ Read the passage and identify the verbs. Discuss why the verbs are all in the past tense. Try changing some of the sentences into the present tense and noting the difference.

▶ Draw attention to some of the more powerful and descriptive verbs used, such as 'the green prairie rippled'.

Sentence construction and punctuation

▶ The passage is excellent for highlighting the use of commas marking grammatical boundaries within sentences.

Word level

Spelling

▶ Find examples of two-syllable words in the text with double consonants in the middle, such as 'ripple, scatter, hammer, alley, cutting, muddy'. Demonstrate by tapping out the syllables and showing where the syllable boundary in each comes (rip – ple, scat – ter).

Vocabulary extension

▶ Select some words from the text and ask children to define them in their own words. Compare and discuss definitions, with a view to refining them. Compare them with dictionary definitions of the same words.

ANSWERS

Thinking back

1 Pa was travelling in a wagon.
2 Laura, Carrie and Mary were waiting for Pa's wagon.
3 Their new house was made of wood.
4 Their new house had just one long room.

Thinking about it

1 a) (open answer) You would probably hear the sounds of buildings being erected (hammering, sawing) people talking and shouting, and the sound of wagons and horses.
   b) (open answer) You would probably see lots of new buildings being erected and people working on them, horse-drawn wagons and carts in the muddy main street, people walking and talking, and, in the distance, the green open prairie.
2 (open answer) You can tell the town is new by all the building that is going on in the main street and by the fact that there is no proper road yet.
3 The prairie surrounds the town.
4 (open answer) It was probably spring or summer, because it mentions young grass in the street and the green prairie.

Thinking it through

1 (open answer) The style of houses, the fact that people are travelling in horse-drawn wagons, and the style of dress are all clues.
2 (open answer)
3 (open answer)
4 (open answer)

▷ *Copymaster* **Describing People**
Children are given six descriptions and six pictures, and are asked to match them up.

Describing People

Name _____   Date _____

Cut out the descriptions.
Stick each one under the correct picture.

Emma has long fair hair and a round face. She is wearing a tee shirt.	Sam has short curly hair. He wears glasses and a tie.	Abdi sucks his thumb. He wears a baseball cap.
Shirleen has dark hair. She wears earrings and a necklace.	Ben has lost a front tooth. He has a scar on his cheek.	Mary likes the sun. She always wears sun glasses.

Book 2 / Copymaster / Unit 1

Focus on Comprehension Teacher's Book 'B'   Text © Louis Fidge 1999   Illustrations © Nelson 1999   Published by Thomas Nelson and Sons Ltd

FURTHER TEACHING OPPORTUNITIES

Text level

Reading comprehension

▶ Relate the poem to children's experiences of time passing. Under what circumstances does it seem to pass quickly? slowly?

▶ Discuss the build-up to parties, the preparation, the anticipation and the waiting. Identify these elements in the poem. Note how the poet accentuates the feeling of time passing slowly.

▶ Draw attention to the way every other line rhymes.

▶ Try and find other poems by James Reeves for comparison and discussion.

Writing composition

▶ Use the structure of the poem for children to write their own 'waiting' poems, building in the repetition of the word waiting. Try it as a class poem first, listing brief phrases, and experimenting by shortening or lengthening sentences, and by asking children to suggest more powerful or expressive verbs.

Sentence level

Grammatical awareness

▶ This poem is good for discussing verb tenses. It is written mainly in the present tense, with the child waiting, but at this moment in time, looking forward to what will happen in the future. Write some sentences in the future tense based on the poem. For example, 'At the party there will be lots of noise. Children will play lots of games.'

Sentence construction and punctuation

▶ Note the use of commas in lists, as in waiting, waiting, waiting. Make up some more lists based on a party theme – lists of food, drink, games, presents, guests.

Word level

Spelling

▶ Select words from the poem with high frequency letter patterns, such as light, hair, floor, tricks. Ask children to suggest other similar words.

Vocabulary extension

▶ Take the rhyming words from the poem. Brainstorm other words that rhyme. On the board build up as big a bank of rhyming words from these as possible.

ANSWERS

Thinking back

1 The poet is waiting for the <u>party</u> to begin.
2 The poet's <u>clothes</u> are trim and tidy.
3 The <u>floor</u> is all shiny.
4 The <u>lights</u> are ablaze.
5 There are plenty of <u>sweetmeats</u>.

Thinking about it

1 a) The poem says the hair is 'just so' with its top-knot in place.
   b) The poem describes the clothes as being 'trim and tidy'.
2 The floor has probably been polished.
3 Sweetmeats and cakes are mentioned.
4 The poet is looking forward to the party to begin, the games, the dancing, the music, the madness, the colour and the noise.
5 (open answer)

Thinking it through

1 (open answer)
2 The poet repeats the line four times. This probably expresses the poet's frustration at having to wait so long.
3 This emphasises how long a wait it seems to be.
4 Two words that give you a clue are – top-knot, sweetmeats
5 (open answer)

⇨ *Copymaster* **It's Today ... Isn't It?**
This is another poem on the theme of waiting for birthdays. It could be used for reading aloud and for comparing with the poem in the unit to discuss similarities and to encourage children to express their opinions.

➡️ It's Today … Isn't It?

Name _____   *Date* _____

**Practise reading the poem. Compare it to the poem in Unit 2.
How are they similar? Which do you like best? Why?**

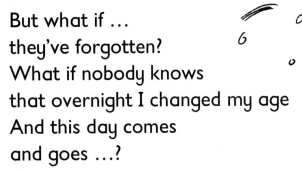

I lie here, still,
hardly breathing
trying to guess the time.
Can I get up now? will they know
that now I'm really nine?

But what if …
they've forgotten?
What if nobody knows
that overnight I changed my age
And this day comes
and goes …?

So would that mean no presents?
No lovely birthday cake?
No cards, no games, no friends for tea?
I hope I'm not awake.

And then I'm roughly shaken
as the twins jump on my bed,
'Get up! Get up! It's half past ten –
Your birthday, sleepy-head!'

Focus on Comprehension Teacher's Book 'B'   Text © Louis Fidge 1999 Illustrations © Nelson 1999   Published by Thomas Nelson and Sons Ltd

FURTHER TEACHING OPPORTUNITIES

Text level

Reading comprehension

▶ Discuss the playscript, asking children to explain the differences between the way it is set out and the way prose is presented. How is dialogue expressed? Who are the characters? How do they know when to speak?

▶ There is no narrator in this script. If there was, how might the narrator set the scene?

▶ Ask children to suggest where the scene is taking part in and what the various characters are doing. How do they come to their conclusions? Is there any evidence?

▶ What impressions are built up of the different characters in the play? How?

Writing composition

▶ Write another scene involving the family. Choose an everyday situation, such as an accident at home, bedtime or a party to base it around.

Sentence level

Grammatical awareness

▶ Take some of the sentences from the play and change the verb so it does not agree with the subject. For example, 'I were only trying to help.' Ask children to identify what is wrong and to articulate their reasoning.

Sentence construction and punctuation

▶ Notice how commas are often used to separate a person's name when it comes at the end of a sentence. 'Did she spill the milk, Dad?'

Word level

Spelling

▶ Have a phoneme challenge. Give the children a list of phonemes, such as 'oa', 'ea', 'ow', 'ou', 'au', 'ur'. Ask children to find at least one word containing each phoneme in the passage.

Vocabulary extension

▶ Ask children to find words from the passage beginning with a particular letter, such as 't'. List them on the board. Discuss how they can be arranged alphabetically, by reference to either the second, third or fourth letter as necessary.

ANSWERS

Thinking back

1 Mr and Mrs Ruggles are the mother and father of the family.
2 Lily Rose was let out of school early.
3 Lily Rose was trying to help her Mum.
4 Mr Ruggles wanted his tea.

Thinking about it

1 Dad is not home at the beginning, because Lily Rose says, 'Here's Dad coming now.'
2 The play takes place in the kitchen of the house. You can tell by the picture.
3 Lily Rose is probably older because she helps with things like ironing, which would be too dangerous for the younger children.
4 It means it's no good getting upset about things going wrong after they've happened.

Thinking it through

1 (open answer)
2 Playscripts are set out clearly so each person knows exactly what they have to say and when they have to say it.
3 A narrator is a storyteller.
4 (open answer)

▷ *Copymaster*   **What Does It Mean?**
Mr Ruggles is always using colloquialisms and strange expressions. Children are asked to rewrite some sentences containing some colloquialisms in their own words.

What Does It Mean?

Name _____   Date _____

Mr Ruggles uses some strange expressions.
Rewrite these in your own words.

1 Mr Ruggles said it was no use **crying over spilt milk** when
   he tore his trousers.

   _____

2 It was **raining cats and dogs**.

   _____

3 Tom's **heart was in his mouth** when he saw the monster.

   _____

4 Mrs Ruggles kept her husband **in the dark** about the problem.

   _____

5 The children **cheered their heads off** at the school sports.

   _____

6 Mr Ruggles **smelt a rat** when his son came in late.

   _____

7 Mr and Mrs Ruggles were **at loggerheads** over buying a new car.

   _____

8 Lily Rose made **a lightning dash** for the exit.

   _____

9 Lily Rose was **the apple of her father's eye**.

   _____

10 When Mrs Ruggles told the children about the holiday
   they were **all ears**.

   _____

Book 2 / Copymaster / Unit 3

Focus on Comprehension Teacher's Book 'B'   Text © Louis Fidge 1999   Illustrations © Nelson 1999   Published by Thomas Nelson and Sons Ltd

FURTHER TEACHING OPPORTUNITIES

Text level

Reading comprehension

▶ How easy is it to predict the content of the article from the headline? Is this always the case? Collect samples of headlines and discuss.

▶ Note how the article is laid out, in paragraphs, and columns. Also draw attention to the use of the opening sentence to set the scene and capture the interest. When reading the article ask children to pick out key phrases and words that convey information.

▶ Discuss the difference between fact and opinion. Note that this article is largely factual.

▶ Take the opportunity of looking together at newspapers, identifying main features including layout, range of information, voice, level of formality, organisation of articles, advertisements and headlines.

Writing composition

▶ Use the article as a model and write newspaper style reports, such as about school events or an incident from a story, including composing headlines, using IT to draft and lay out the reports, organising the writing into paragraphs.

Sentence level

Grammatical awareness

▶ Identify the verbs and list them, discussing the merits of each, thinking of suitable substitutes if possible.

▶ Find some adverbs in the passage, such as seriously, severely, completely. Discuss how these add to the meaning of the verb. This can be emphasised by reading the sentence and leaving the adverb out.

Sentence construction and punctuation

▶ Notice how a comma is used to separate the actual dialogue, from the person who said it. Find an example in the text.

Word level

Spelling

▶ Use the regular verbs in the passage for suffixing practice with 's', 'ing' and 'ed' (knocks, knocking, knocked).

▶ Find examples of irregular past tenses in the passage and learn them (struck, blew, heard, gave, and so on).

Vocabulary extension

▶ Ask children to define some of the more interesting words in the text, such as cylinder, demolish. Compare their definition with dictionary definitions.

ANSWERS

Thinking back

1 The explosion was caused by a gas cylinder exploding.
2 Tim O'Donovan was injured.
3 The accident happened at Farr's Factory in Oakley Road, Bedford.
4 A local resident reported the accident.
5 The fire fighters got to the scene first.
6 Mr O'Donovan received wounds in his stomach and groin.

Thinking about it

Mr O'Donovan was demolishing an old building.
He struck a gas cylinder.
The gas cylinder exploded.
A local resident telephoned for help.
The fire fighters arrived and rescued Mr O'Donovan.
Mr O'Donovan was taken to hospital.

Thinking it through

1 (open answer)
2 (open answer) Headlines are usually written in capitals to make them stand out.
3 (open answers)
4 (open answer)

➡ *Copymaster* **Read All About It!**
Children are given eight newspaper headlines and the first sentences from the accompanying articles. Their task is to decide which goes with which.

⇨ Read All About It!

Name _____ Date _____

Match each newspaper headline (1–8) to one of the reports
(A–H). Write the answers at the bottom of the page.

1 | **JAM ON MOTORWAY**   2 | **GRAN GETS THE GORILLA**

3 | **OLD CROCKS ON SHOW**   4 | **FACING THE MUSIC**

5 | **THE BIG SELL-OUT**   6 | **STORMS STRIKE**

7 | **HAT-TRICK FOR HENRY**   8 | **UP UP AND AWAY**

A | 56 year-old Margaret Smith, a grandmother, suddenly found herself face to face with an escaped gorilla yesterday.

B | All the tickets for the big match were sold out by lunch-time yesterday.

C | Tibbles, a pet cat, stowed away in the basket of a hot air balloon, and found himself above the clouds last Tuesday.

D | A lorry containing jars of jam overturned on the motorway last week, spilling its load all over the road.

E | The choir from Park Farm Junior School got through to the finals of the Fordham Music Festival on Thursday.

F | Weather forecasters are being blamed for not giving a warning about the storms that struck last night.

G | Elton's main striker, Justin Henry, grabbed a hat-trick of goals against local rivals, Grimthorp, on Wednesday.

H | Valuable crockery, dating back to the 17th century, went on show at Market Museum today.

Answers

1 ___   2 ___   3 ___   4 ___   5 ___   6 ___   7 ___   8 ___

Book 2 / Copymaster / Unit 4

Focus on Comprehension Teacher's Book 'B'   Text © Louis Fidge 1999 Illustrations © Nelson 1999   Published by Thomas Nelson and Sons Ltd

FURTHER TEACHING OPPORTUNITIES

Text level

Reading comprehension

▶ Discuss with the class the function of this text. Draw attention to the way it is set out, the clear headings, a list of what is needed, the rules and explanation clearly set out. Are the instructions helpful? Do children think they could play the game now?

Writing composition

▶ Ask children to use the text as a model and to write instructions for playing a simple game like noughts and crosses or conkers. Look at the texts once they are written and comment together on how they might be improved, such as by using sub-headings, numbering.

Sentence level

Grammatical awareness

▶ Explain that verbs in instructions are usually written in the present tense. Check to see if this is the case.

Sentence construction and punctuation

▶ Ask children why they think the three headings in the text are all posed as questions.

Word level

Spelling

▶ Find examples of the homophones 'two' and 'to' in the text. Ask children to make up sentences showing they know how to use them. Do the same for the word 'too'. In a similar way, work on 'their' and 'there', and 'piece' and 'peace'.

Vocabulary extension

▶ Ask children to find words from the passage beginning with a particular letter, such as 'r'. List them on the board. Discuss how they can be arranged alphabetically, by reference to either the second, third or fourth letter, as necessary.

ANSWERS

Thinking back

1 Three-Hole is a game for two players.
2 The children in Guyana play Three-Hole a lot.
3 Each player needs some marbles to play.
4 You need to make three holes in the ground.

Thinking about it

1 Three-Hole is an outside game because you need to make holes in the ground or sand.
2 It is true you do not need a lot of equipment. You basically just need some marbles.
3 The weather in Guyana is often hot, because the ground is dusty and dry.
4 The game is won by one player getting three marbles into the holes before his or her opponent.

Thinking it through

1 (open answer) The headings help break the text up and make it easier to follow.
2 (open answer) A good way to check the accuracy and clarity of the text would be to try out the instructions and see if they are easy to understand and if they work.
3 (open answer) Games have to have rules to help prevent cheating, and so that everyone knows exactly what to do.
4 (open answer)

⇨ *Copymaster*   **Three-Hole**

This poem, by John Agard, complements the unit. It describes the game in poetic form. It could be used for comparison with the instructional language of the text in the unit. The poem is expressed in non-standard English.

⇨ Three-Hole

Name _____   Date _____

**Read this poem about a marble game played by children
in Guyana.**

Three-Hole
is the name
of a marble game
we got in Guyana.

Is fun to play
and not hard.
Just dig three lil holes
in you yard
or the sand
by you gate.

The aim straight

for first-hole
    second-hole
        third-hole.

If you lucky
and you marble
go in all three holes
one two three

Then is you chance
to knock you friend marble.
Send it flying for a dance.
When marble burst then fun start

Focus on Comprehension Teacher's Book 'B'   Text © Louis Fidge 1999 Illustrations © Nelson 1999   Published by Thomas Nelson and Sons Ltd

FURTHER TEACHING OPPORTUNITIES

Text level

Reading comprehension

▶ It would be helpful to set this 'letter' in context, by reviewing what children know about Vikings and their lifestyle. The 'letter' provides some insight into this. For instance, we can learn a lot about dress, weapons, eating habits and other aspects of life from it. Concentrate on each of these aspects one at a time and ask children to suggest what can be discovered. Some things can be learnt by inference, for instance, roles were clearly defined: only men went raiding.

▶ The text may also be seen as an explanatory text too, with an introduction, followed by explanation and detail, much of it couched in semi-formal language and written in the passive voice (although the letter must be read with tongue-in-cheek!) It would be interesting to compare the style of the letter and its features with letters typically sent home from your school.

Writing composition

▶ Ask children to make notes on what they have discovered about aspects of Viking life.

▶ Have fun making up imaginary letters to parents about school visits and trips in the style of Eric Bloodaxe's letter.

Sentence level

Grammatical awareness

▶ The way people sign letters is good for discussing use of adverbs, (such as sincerely, faithfully). Consider other types of letters and how people might sign them. For example, Eric could have signed off 'bloodthirstily'!

Sentence construction and punctuation

▶ Notice the differing uses of the comma in the letter.

Word level

Spelling

▶ Look at the word 'educational'. Discuss the root word and how the suffix 'al' has been added. Ask children to suggest other words with this suffix and study them; for example, sensational, national, occasional, accidental, comical, natural, signal, musical. Consider words that are suffixed with -ary, -ic, -ship, -hood, -ness, -ment in a similar way.

Vocabulary extension

▶ Explore and discuss words that imply gender, such as son/daughter, prince/princess. Use the word 'son' from the text as a starting point. Focus first on terms relating to humans and then widen it to terms for male and female animals.

ANSWERS

Thinking back

1 The letter is about a <u>Viking raid</u>.
2 It is from <u>Eric Bloodaxe</u>.
3 The letter is to <u>parents</u>.
4 The trip is to <u>The Baltic Sea</u>.
5 The trip will take about <u>six months</u>.

Thinking about it

1 The purpose of the trip is to develop the educational experiences of Viking warriors.
2 (open answer) The Vikings were known to be a war-like and aggressive nation. Bad behaviour would therefore be expected of them.
3 The items of clothing listed are chain mail, iron helmet, leather tunic, boots, cloak, mittens or gloves, spare trousers.
4 Weapons to be taken are an axe, a knife, an ash wood spear, a double-edged sword, a large round shield, and a bow and arrows.
5 (open answer) Eric Bloodaxe is probably the chief or leader.

Thinking it through

1 (open answer)
2 (open answer)
3 (open answer)

⇨ *Copymaster*
The Development of Boats with Sails

This explanatory article is in the form of a cloze procedure. Children are asked to predict the missing words using a variety of cues.

The Development of Boats with Sails

Name _____   Date _____

Read this passage about the development
of sailing ships. Think of a suitable word
to fill in each gap.

The first boats were logs or _____ trunks. At some _____ it

was discovered that it was _____ to move a boat along in the

same direction _____ the wind. All that was _____ was a

sail of some sort _____ catch the wind to use _____ power

more effectively.

The Ancient Egyptians had _____ that used both oars and huge

_____. At _____ their ships were _____ used on the River

Nile, but _____ they went _____ on the open sea.

The Greeks and Romans _____ a kind of ship _____ a

galley. These were fighting ships used _____ battles. They had

oars _____ a sail. The rowing was done _____ slaves.

At about this _____ another kind of ship was developed

_____ was called a 'round' ship. These _____ were used

for carrying cargo. The first round ships had only _____ mast with

one great sail. _____ the number of sails was increased to

_____ them go faster.

The Vikings, who were great explorers and _____, used ships

with sails. By 800 A.D. _____ had ships with large square sails,

capable of _____ great distances.

Book 2 / Copymaster / Unit 6

Focus on Comprehension Teacher's Book 'B'   Text © Louis Fidge 1999 Illustrations © Nelson 1999   Published by Thomas Nelson and Sons Ltd

FURTHER TEACHING OPPORTUNITIES

Text level

Reading comprehension

▶ Discuss the theme of the poem and practise reading whilst accentuating the rhythmic element of the train.

▶ Identify patterns of rhyme in it (such as rhyming couplets). Look for clues which suggest this is an older poem (language use, archaic words).

▶ Draw attention to the descriptive and figurative language used, such as the use of simile: 'charging along like troops into battle'.

▶ Point out the name of the poet and find out more about other poems or books written by him.

Writing composition

▶ Discuss how things (people, animals, types of transport) move, encouraging the use of similes, adjectives and adverbs. Pick a theme, brainstorm ideas, note them on the board. Convert the ideas into a poem.

Sentence level

Grammatical awareness

▶ Take the adjectives 'fast' and 'thick' from the poem. Discuss how adjectives can be compared, such as fast, faster, fastest. Compare other adjectives in a similar way, noting what changes are needed, when suffixes are added. Explain that when the adjective consists of more than two syllables, we usually preface it with the words 'more' and 'most'. Ask children to think of examples.

Sentence construction and punctuation

▶ Experiment with the use of word order in the poem. Note that some re-orderings destroy meaning and that some make sense but change meaning.

Word level

Spelling

▶ This poem is good for looking at how pluralisation of nouns affects their spelling, such as troop – troops, fairy – fairies, ditch – ditches.

Vocabulary extension

▶ Discuss the way in which the poet has avoided overused words and selected more descriptive words, such as 'whistle' by, instead of 'go' by. Encourage children to find alternatives to words like 'got', 'nice', 'good', 'then' in their own writing.

ANSWERS

Thinking back

1 The train goes faster than <u>witches</u>.
2 The train passes through <u>meadows</u>.
3 Painted <u>stations</u> whistle by.
4 The child is gathering <u>brambles</u>.
5 A <u>tramp</u> stands and gazes at the train.
6 On the road there is a man in a <u>cart</u>.

Thinking about it

1 (open answer)
2 'In the wink of an eye' means very quickly.
3 Here are some of the things seen from the train: bridges, houses, hedges, ditches, meadows, horses, cattle, hill, plain, stations, a child, a mill.
4 This means to go past very quickly.
5 Each thing is only seen briefly then not seen again.
6 (open answer)

Thinking it through

1 It is an old poem because steam trains are no longer common. The picture also gives you a clue that it is not a modern poem.
2 a) There are two verses in the poem.
   b) There are eight lines in each verse.
   c) Yes, it is a rhyming poem.
   d) witches – ditches; battle – cattle; plain – rain; eye – by; scrambles – brambles; gazes – daisies; road – load.
   e) (open answer)
3 (open answers)
4 Robert Louis Stevenson wrote the poem. (open answer)

▭▶ *Copymaster* **Night Mail**
This extract from the famous W H Auden poem complements the poem in the unit, both in style and theme, and presents many opportunities for rhythmic reading and for comparison.

 # Night Mail

This is the night mail crossing the Border,
Bringing the cheque and the postal order,

Letter for the rich, letters for the poor,
The shop at the corner, the girl next door.

Pulling up at Beattock, a steady climb:
The gradient's against her, but she's on time.

Past cotton-grass and moorland boulder,
Shovelling white steam over her shoulder,

Snorting noisily, she passes
Silent miles of wind-bent grasses.

Birds turn their heads as she approaches,
Stare from bushes at her blank-faced coaches.

Sheep dogs cannot turn her course;
They slumber on with paws across.

In the farm she passes no one wakes
But the jug in the bedroom gently shakes

► Practise reading this poem. Notice the strong rhythm.

► Compare it with Robert Louis Stevenson's poem in Unit 7.

► They both have the same theme. What is it?

► Do the poems have anything else in common?

► Which poem do you prefer? Why?

Book 2 / Copymaster / Unit 7

Focus on Comprehension Teacher's Book 'B'   Text © Louis Fidge 1999 Illustrations © Nelson 1999   Published by Thomas Nelson and Sons Ltd

FURTHER TEACHING OPPORTUNITIES

Text level

Reading comprehension

▶ This is an excellent passage for exploring how the author creates interest and builds up tension from the outset (by the use of questions, short sentences and descriptive language). Notice how the picture of the Iron Man is gradually built up. Ask children to respond to the text. How do they feel when they read it? What pictures come into their minds? What questions does it raise? How will the story continue?

▶ Discuss what sort of a story this passage might come from. (Science fiction, ghost story, adventure?) What other story types are there?

Writing composition

▶ This story begs to be continued! Ask for suggestions on what might happen. List ideas. Build up possibilities for different chapters for an 'Iron Man' book.

Sentence level

Grammatical awareness

▶ Read the passage again, focussing especially on the descriptive language. Identify the adjectives, and the use of similes.

Sentence construction and punctuation

▶ The passage is full of opportunities for looking at the use and significance of punctuation, the use of capitals for proper nouns, emphasis, sentence beginnings; the use of commas for marking grammatical boundaries, in lists; the use of question and exclamation marks.

Word level

Spelling

▶ Use the word 'cliff' to discuss words ending in either 'f' or 'ff'. List as many words as possible on the board from children's suggestions. Experiment and find out what happens when suffixes are added, such as shelf – shelves, cliff – cliffs, stiff – stiffly.

Vocabulary extension

▶ Play the 'suffix challenge'. Invite children to find words in the text that have been suffixed. Explore what the root words are and how the suffix has changed the meaning and, in some cases, the spelling of the root word.

ANSWERS

Thinking back

The Iron Man came to the <u>top</u> of the cliff. Nobody knew where he had come <u>from</u>. Nobody knew <u>how</u> he was made. He was taller than a <u>house</u>. His <u>head</u> was shaped like a dustbin. His <u>ears</u> turned this way and that. The Iron Man could hear the <u>sea</u>. His eyes were like <u>headlamps</u>. His eyes changed colour. He had <u>never</u> seen the sea before. There was a <u>strong</u> wind. It made the Iron Man sway. The Iron Man <u>stepped</u> off the cliff. He <u>fell</u> down with a loud noise.

Thinking about it

1 The passage takes place on a cliff top by the sea.
2 There was a very strong wind.
3 (open answer)
4 (open answer)
5 (open answer)

Thinking it through

1 (open answer)
2 (open answer) It probably means the wind whistled through his fingers and made a kind of singing noise.
3 (open answer) Writing it this way makes the reader take note and realise that it was a loud, drawn-out noise.
4 (open answer)

⇨ *Copymaster* **The Metal Monster**
This copymaster is in the form of a sequencing activity. It consists of several sentences which make up a story, echoing that of the Iron Man.

⇨ The Metal Monster

Name _____   Date _____

Cut out these sentences. Put
them in order to tell a story.
Stick them in your book.

When you have done that,
write a few more sentences in
your book and continue it.

The children heard the noise and looked up.

One evening Ben and Emma were walking along the beach.

Standing on the edge of the cliff was a huge metal monster.

Slowly the children bent down to take a closer look.

It was about to step off the edge!

A rock came tumbling down the cliff.

Ben and Emma stared in wonder as the monster landed at their feet.

Crash! Bang! Thud! The metal monster came crashing down.

Their mouths dropped open in surprise.

They could not believe their eyes.

Book 2 / Copymaster / Unit 8

Focus on Comprehension Teacher's Book 'B'   Text © Louis Fidge 1999 Illustrations © Nelson 1999   Published by Thomas Nelson and Sons Ltd

FURTHER TEACHING OPPORTUNITIES

Text level

Reading comprehension

▶ Discuss the way this explanatory text is structured, with an introduction, followed by a number of paragraphs answering specific questions relating to bats. Note too, that the explanation is exclusively in the present tense, and is fairly factual, using a passive formal style. Illustrations are used to complement the text.

▶ Consider how helpful the headings are for scanning the page and getting an immediate idea of what the text is all about.

▶ The text is also useful for considering paragraphing and discussing how each paragraph deals with one particular theme or topic only.

Writing composition

▶ This text is ideal for practising note-taking skills. Ask children to go through it and jot down only key words or phrases from it.

Sentence level

Grammatical awareness

▶ Take the adjective 'clean' from the passage. Discuss how adjectives can be compared, such as clean, cleaner, cleanest. Select a range of other adjectives and experiment with these in a similar way, noting what changes are needed, when suffixes are added.

Sentence construction and punctuation

▶ Take the word 'don't' from the text and examine how it has been contracted, how the apostrophe is used and what letter is missing. Ask children to look in reading books for other examples of contractions and to write them in their longer form.

▶ If appropriate, introduce the use of the apostrophe for marking possession, using the word 'bat' as a starting point (such as the bat's wings). Find examples in reading books and discuss how the apostrophe is used.

Word level

Spelling

▶ Notice the way the word 'echo' has been pluralised. Think of other nouns ending in 'o' and explore how they are written in the plural. 'Echo' is also interesting in the way the 'ch' makes a hard sound. Think of other words using the 'ch' in this way.

Vocabulary extension

▶ Ask children to define words from the text in their own words. Impose constraints, such as restricting the number of words in which to do it.

ANSWERS

Thinking back
1 There are over 1000 types of bats.
2 Bats look like mice with wings. They have furry bodies, big ears and big eyes.
3 Bats often live in caves or roost in trees. Some bats make their homes in buildings.
4 They usually catch insects while they are flying.
5 Bats use their ears more than their eyes.

Thinking about it
1 Bats are clean animals because they don't like dusty buildings.
2 A mammal is a warm-blooded animal that gives birth to live young.
3 You don't see many bats during the day because they usually only come out at night to hunt.
4 Bats give off high-pitched squeaks to prevent them from bumping into things. The squeaks bounce off objects like an echo and tell the bats how near they are to things.

Thinking it through
1 (open answer)
2 (open answer)
3 (open answer)
4 Bats eat insects and fruit.

▢▶ *Copymaster* **Hamsters**
Children are given some information about hamsters in note form and are asked to expand it into a paragraph of proper sentences.

⇨ Hamsters

Name _____ *Date* _____

Here are some notes on hamsters. Use the notes to help you write a paragraph of proper sentences about them.

Length:	Up to 15 cm
Found in:	Europe and Asia.
Home:	Burrows or underground holes
Appearance:	Plump body with short limbs. Thick, soft golden fur on back. Greyish-white fur on belly.
Young:	Has up to six litters a year. Each litter up to 12 babies.
Food:	Carries food back to burrow in pouches in cheeks. Can carry up to half body weight in pouches.

HAMSTERS

_____

_____

_____

_____

_____

_____

_____

_____

_____

Focus on Comprehension Teacher's Book 'B'   Text © Louis Fidge 1999 Illustrations © Nelson 1999   Published by Thomas Nelson and Sons Ltd

FURTHER TEACHING OPPORTUNITIES

Text level

Reading comprehension
- ▶ Encourage the children to have fun reading this poem aloud, with expression, taking account of the punctuation.
- ▶ The poem is interesting in that it doesn't follow the same rhyming pattern. Find and discuss the rhyming sentences, such as 'Don't put toffee in my coffee.'
- ▶ Ask children from whose perspective the poem is written. Can they empathise with the theme? Ask them for their opinion of the poem.
- ▶ Find other Michael Rosen poems to read and compare.

Writing composition
- ▶ Use the rhyming sentence idea for writing 'silly' poems on rules in school.

Sentence level

Grammatical awareness
- ▶ The poem is full of commands or orders which use the imperative. Point out that the instructions are aimed at 'you' although the pronoun is implicit and never stated.

Sentence construction and punctuation
- ▶ Take the words 'don't' and 'they'll' from the poem and examine how they have been contracted, how the apostrophe is used and what letters are missing. Ask children to look in reading books for other examples of contractions and to write them in their longer form.

Word level

Spelling
- ▶ Have 'phoneme hunts'. Provide the children with a list of phonemes, such as 'ea', 'oo', 'u-e', 'ee', 'ou'. Ask them to find words in the poem containing the phonemes and to suggest other words with the same letter patterns.

Vocabulary extension
- ▶ Try substituting alternatives for some of the verbs used.

ANSWERS

Thinking back
1 Don't pull <u>faces</u>.
2 Don't be rude at <u>school</u>.
3 Don't put toffee in my <u>coffee</u>.
4 Don't pour gravy on the <u>baby</u>.
5 Don't put confetti in the <u>spaghetti</u>.
6 Don't squash peas on your <u>knees</u>.

Thinking about it
1 (open answer)
2 (open answer)
3 (open answer)
4 (open answer)

Thinking it through
1 (open answer)
2 (open answer)
3 (open answer)
4 (open answer)

➡ *Copymaster* Rhyme Time
The poem contains many rhyming sentences. The copymaster picks up this theme. The children are asked to complete pairs of rhyming words from cryptic clues.

 Rhyme Time

Name _____   Date _____

What do you call a young hen that is ill?

A sick chick!

Think of a suitable word to complete each answer to make it rhyme.

1	Extra wig	spare	hair
2	Unhappy mother	glum	_____
3	A metal container	tin	_____
4	Recall the last month	remember	_____
5	Tiny round object for throwing	small	_____
6	Immobile lorry	stuck	_____
7	The cleverest painter	smartest	_____
8	An overweight rodent	fat	_____
9	Black stain	dark	_____
10	Animal doctor	pet	_____
11	Unusual type of fish	odd	_____
12	Brief idea	short	_____
13	Wooden limb	peg	_____
14	Cut two times	slice	_____

Focus on Comprehension Teacher's Book 'B'   Text © Louis Fidge 1999 Illustrations © Nelson 1999   Published by Thomas Nelson and Sons Ltd

FURTHER TEACHING OPPORTUNITIES

Text level

Reading comprehension

▶ Discuss how information about the characters is built up through dialogue in the passage. In what sense do all the characters have something in common?

▶ Is it possible to tell where the story is set from this brief passage? Are there any clues at all? Ask children to supply further details, based on their own knowledge of the book or film. Encourage them to express their personal opinions of the book.

Writing composition

▶ Children could be asked to invent other imaginary characters met along the way, who each have something wrong with them, and to write a character profile for each.

▶ Ask children to write about things that worry or frighten them.

Sentence level

Grammatical awareness

▶ Use the adverb 'thoughtfully' from the passage to focus on adverbs that might describe how people say things. Ask children to suggest appropriate adverbs to accompany the verb 'to speak' (such as to speak loudly, softly, haltingly).

Sentence construction and punctuation

▶ The passage is full of dialogue. Focus on the punctuation conventions used in writing dialogue down.

Word level

Spelling

▶ Find words in the text that have been prefixed. Identify the prefixes and root words, and discuss any changes in meaning that is caused by adding a prefix. Lead on to a consideration of the prefix 'al' as in 'always, almighty, altogether'. How many words can children think of? What happens to the spelling of 'all' when used as a prefix?

Vocabulary extension

▶ Notice how the noun 'coward' is changed into an adjective by the addition of the suffix 'ly'. Think of further examples of nouns or verbs that can be made into adjectives by the addition of the following suffixes: 'able' – washable; 'ful' – hopeful; 'ing' – shocking; 'like' – childlike; 'ic' – heroic; 'worthy' – roadworthy.

ANSWERS

Thinking back

1 The Scarecrow said that the King of Beasts should not be a coward.
2 The Tin Woodman said that perhaps the Lion had heart disease.
3 The Scarecrow said that his head was stuffed with straw.
4 The Cowardly Lion asked if Oz could give him courage.

Thinking about it

1 The Lion is a coward, the Tin Man has no heart, and the Scarecrow has no brains.
2 Each character hopes that the Great Oz will solve their problems.
3 The Lion says it makes him unhappy and he cries.
4 Whenever the Lion is in danger his heart begins to beat fast.

Thinking it through

1 The Great Oz is a wizard.
2 (open answer) Wizards can cast spells and change things.
3 (open answer) A coward is a person without courage.
4 (open answer)

➡ *Copymaster* **Cinderella Playlet**

Children are expected to read this short playlet, and complete the missing lines of the narrator by using information and inferences based on the text.

Cinderella Playlet

Name _____   Date _____

**Read the short play.
Write the script for
the narrator.**

Narrator: _____

Cinderella: Sweep, sweep, sweep! That's all I do. I wish something
exciting would happen.

Narrator: _____

Fairy: I have come to help you. Would you like to meet a prince?

Cinderella: Yes please! Can you arrange it straight away?

Fairy: That's no problem. I'll just wave my magic wand and …

Narrator: _____

Prince: How did I get here?

Fairy: There's no time to explain. Let me introduce you to Cinderella.

Prince: Enchanted to meet you. You are just the person I've been
looking for.

Cinderella: You're the Prince of my dreams!

Prince: You certainly do a good job cleaning this place. I'm sure
you'll keep my castle nice and clean, too.

Cinderella: Clean your castle? That's not what I had in mind! Fairy
Godmother! Come back here at once!

Narrator: _____

_____

Focus on Comprehension Teacher's Book 'B'   Text © Louis Fidge 1999 Illustrations © Nelson 1999   Published by Thomas Nelson and Sons Ltd

FURTHER TEACHING OPPORTUNITIES

Text level

Reading comprehension

▶ Notice how this poem is set out and the way it does not stick to many usual conventions of poetry or punctuation. Consider in what ways this might be termed a 'poem'.

▶ Consider what clues there are that tell the reader the poem is set in a different culture.

▶ From whose perspective is the poem written? How is it possible to tell?

Writing composition

▶ Ask children to talk about the sounds and thoughts that impinge on them as they lay in bed at night, before going to sleep. Use this as a way into writing a list poem on the theme of 'I love the...' based on the senses (smells, sounds, feelings). Stress that the poem does not have to rhyme.

Sentence level

Grammatical awareness

▶ Take the adjectives 'warm' and 'fresh' from the poem. Discuss how adjectives can be compared (For example, warm, warmer, warmest). Select a range of other adjectives and experiment with these in a similar way, noting what changes are needed, when suffixes are added.

▶ Compare adjectives on a scale of intensity (such as hot, warm, tepid, lukewarm, chilly, cold).

Sentence construction and punctuation

▶ This poems presents many opportunities for discussing punctuation, or lack of it! Explain that sometimes poets use poetic licence and ignore conventional rules. Read through the poem and discuss where punctuation marks could have been used and where unusual things have been included such as the use of the ampersand, lower case and capital letters used unusually.

▶ The poem also reflects language widely used in the Caribbean, which does not follow the rules of standard English such as the lack of agreement between subject and verb. Find examples of things like this and discuss.

Word level

Spelling

▶ Have 'phoneme hunts'. Give the children a list of phonemes such as 'ea'. Ask them to find words in the poem containing the phonemes and to suggest other words with the same letter patterns.

Vocabulary extension

▶ There are some words in the text that are peculiar to the Caribbean that children might not know. Ask them to suggest possible meanings for these.

ANSWERS

Thinking back

1 The poet's mum does the baking on Friday nights.
2 The poet is in bed when he smells the baking.
3 He dreams he is jumping from a jamoon tree.
4 He dreams he beats Calton.
5 He dreams he catches the biggest fish in the world.

Thinking about it

1 'zzzz' is the sound of someone sleeping.
2 a) 'I'll meet a kitchen table laden with bread' means that he will see a table packed with bread.
  b) The smell 'puts him to sleep' means that as he goes to sleep the smell of baking is in his nostrils.
3 Friday night is special because this is when his mum does all her baking.

Thinking it through

1 (open answer)
2 (open answer)
3 (open answer)
4 (open answer) The poet does not use many punctuation marks or capital letters for proper nouns. Sometimes the subject and verb of the sentences do not agree.

▷ Copymaster   Windy Nights

This famous poem by Robert Louis Stevenson is based on the theme of night, and can be used for comparison with the Caribbean poem in the unit. (It can also be used to compare with the other Robert Louis Stevenson poem in Unit 7.)

 Windy Nights

Name _____   Date _____

Read this poem about night-time.
Think of a suitable illustration to go with it.

Windy Nights

Whenever the moon and stars are set.
Whenever the wind is high,
All night long in the dark and wet,
A man goes riding by.
Late in the night when the fires are out,
Why does he gallop and gallop about?

Whenever the trees are crying aloud,
And ships are tossed at sea,
By, on the highway, low and loud,
By at the gallop goes he.
By at the gallop he goes, and then
By he comes back at the gallop again.

By Robert Louis Stevenson

Book 2 / Copymaster / Unit 12
Focus on Comprehension Teacher's Book 'B'   Text © Louis Fidge 1999 Illustrations © Nelson 1999   Published by Thomas Nelson and Sons Ltd

FURTHER TEACHING OPPORTUNITIES

Text level

Reading comprehension

▶ Read the passage and consider what can be learnt about the two main characters, Grace and her Nana. What sort of people were they? What sort of relationship did they have? How did Nana use the visit to the theatre to encourage Grace?

Writing composition

▶ Ask the children to write about ambitions they have.

Sentence level

Grammatical awareness

▶ Ask children how Grace must have felt at various points through the passage and to supply appropriate adjectives to describe her feelings.

Sentence construction and punctuation

▶ Use some of the nouns in the passage as the starting point for considering the use of possessive apostrophes such as Grace's Nana = the Nana of Grace; the dancer's tutu = the tutu belonging to the dancer.

Word level

Spelling

▶ There are some interesting words that can be used as starting points. The word 'island' is useful for discussing silent letters, small words within long words or mnemonics such as an island is land surrounded by water. 'Tutu' and 'ballet' are both 'loan' words which derive from other countries.

Vocabulary extension

▶ Ask children to define some of the words in the text (such as audition, vote, theatre), using dictionaries to help if necessary

ANSWERS

Thinking back

1 Grace was unhappy because <u>some children said she couldn't be Peter Pan in her school play</u>.
2 Nana told Grace that she could <u>be anything she wanted</u>.
3 Nana took Grace to the <u>theatre to see the ballet</u>.
4 In the ballet, the part of Juliet was played by <u>Rosalie</u>.
5 After the ballet <u>Grace pretended she was a ballet dancer</u>.
6 All the children voted for <u>Grace</u>.

Thinking about it

1 The children were unkind because they said Grace could not be Peter Pan in the play. They said it was because she was black and because she was a girl.
2 (open answer) Nana meant that there was nothing Grace could not do or achieve if she tried hard enough and wanted it badly enough.
3 (open answer) Grace saw that a young black girl had become a star ballet dancer, which gave her the confidence to try again for the part of Peter Pan.

Thinking it through

1 (open answer)
2 Grace was determined because she didn't just give up.
3 (open answer) Nana was an understanding and kind person. She didn't like Grace feeling upset and wanted to give her the confidence to keep trying.
4 a) An audition is a hearing to try out a performer to see how well they can perform or act.
  b) A tutu is a short skirt worn by ballet dancers.
  c) A ballet is a dance or performance set to music.

⇨ *Copymaster*
What Are They Good At?
In the story Grace shows that she is good at acting. This copymaster asks children to consider what skills are needed by people doing a variety of different sorts of jobs.

What Are They Good At?

Name _____   *Date* _____

List three skills that would be needed to do each job below.

For example, a doctor would need:

► to be well trained

► to like people

► to be prepared to work long hours

a teacher

a hairdresser

a builder

a vet

a shop assistant

a pop singer

Focus on Comprehension Teacher's Book 'B'   Text © Louis Fidge 1999   Illustrations © Nelson 1999   Published by Thomas Nelson and Sons Ltd

FURTHER TEACHING OPPORTUNITIES

Text level

Reading comprehension

▶ Discuss the reasons why the hen is portrayed as being an anthropomorphic character. How does this portrayal help the reader? Consider that the author might be wanting to draw attention to the living conditions of hens in factory farming situations, and making a moral point.

▶ What can be learnt about the life in the 'factory'. What are the advantages and disadvantages? How does the setting influence the attitudes of Brown Hen and the others?

Writing composition

▶ What dilemma is Brown Hen faced with at the end? Ask children to predict what might happen next and to continue the story in their own ways. Compare and contrast different endings.

Sentence level

Grammatical awareness

▶ Use the passage to understand how some words can be changed in particular ways and others cannot. For example, experiment by changing verb endings, pluralising words. Discuss what this tells the reader about word classes.

Sentence construction and punctuation

▶ Find an example of brackets being used in the text and discuss their purpose.

Word level

Spelling

▶ Find the words 'warm' and 'want' in the text. Notice how the 'a' sounds like an 'o' in them. Ask children to supply other 'wa' words and see if they fit the pattern. Find examples of 'wo' words in a dictionary (such as in 'word' and 'work') and notice how the 'or' sounds like 'er'.

Vocabulary extension

▶ Talk about animals and their young (duck – ducklings, for example) and discuss how diminutives are sometimes formed by the addition of suffixes like 'ling'.

ANSWERS

Thinking back

1 Brown Hen never saw the stars.
2 A machine tipped food into a tray.
3 When Brown Hen laid an egg it rolled away down a chute.
4 Brown Hen got bored.
5 One night the door of her cage popped wide open.

Thinking about it

1 (open answer) Some advantages were that the hen house was safe and warm, and food was provided. Some disadvantages were that the house was full of other hens, there was no real light, the hens were indoors all the time and it was boring.
2 (open answer) She probably got fed up because she could not really move about and there was nothing to do.
3 The other hens told her to shut up because she had nothing to complain about. She was well-fed and warm.
4 (open answer) It was probably the farmer or one of his helpers.

Thinking it through

1 (open answer)
2 (open answer)
3 (open answer)
4 (open answer)

▢▶ *Copymaster*
Advantages and Disadvantages
The question of factory farming is implicitly addressed in the story in the unit. This copymaster asks children to think of the advantages and disadvantages of four topics familiar to them.

Advantages and Disadvantages

Name _____   Date _____

There are good and bad points about most things.

Think of at least three advantages and disadvantages for each of the following:

	Advantages	Disadvantages
school		
wearing new clothes		
having a car		
being famous		

Focus on Comprehension Teacher's Book 'B'   Text © Louis Fidge 1999 Illustrations © Nelson 1999   Published by Thomas Nelson and Sons Ltd

FURTHER TEACHING OPPORTUNITIES

Text level

Reading comprehension

▶ Discuss the way the text is divided into paragraphs. As a way of identifying key themes, ask children to try and supply a suitable heading for each paragraph that summarises the main point of each.

Writing composition

▶ Encourage the children to make notes on the passage, recording only key words and phrases.

Sentence level

Grammatical awareness

▶ Find all the verbs in the passage. Notice that in this explanatory text they are all in the present tense.

▶ Use the passage to understand how some words can be changed in particular ways and others cannot (for example, experiment by changing verb endings, pluralising words). Discuss what this tells the reader about word classes.

Sentence construction and punctuation

▶ Use the passage to help children understand how the grammar of a sentence alters when the sentence type is altered, when, for example, a statement is made into a question. ('Whales breathe air through their lungs' becomes 'Do whales breathe air through their lungs?') or a positive statement is made into a negative statement ('Whales are warm-blooded animals' becomes 'Whales are not warm-blooded animals').

Word level

Spelling

▶ Explore the occurrence of the letters 'k' and 'v' in words, starting with words from the passage. Deduce some of the conventions for using them at the beginnings and endings of words, and in the middle of words.

Vocabulary extension

▶ A group of whales is called a school. Discuss other collective nouns related to animals.

ANSWERS

Thinking back

1 A whale is not a fish. It is a <u>mammal</u>.
2 Baby whales are not hatched from eggs but are born <u>alive</u>.
3 When a whale needs to breathe it <u>comes to the surface</u>.
4 Under their skins whales have a thick layer of '<u>blubber</u>'.
5 To help them swim, whales have <u>fins and strong tails</u>.
6 A group of whales is called a <u>school</u>.

Thinking about it

1 Whales use a blow hole to breathe through.
2 Whales have little valves on their blow holes to prevent them breathing in water.
3 Blubber is important to keep whales warm.
4 The largest type of whale is the Blue Whale.
5 Whales tend to travel around in groups, called schools.
6 (open answer) Whales probably like to travel around in groups because they are sociable, friendly animals.

Thinking it through

1 (open answer) A mammal is a warm-blooded creature that gives birth to live babies and feeds them on milk.
2 (open answer) It means that whales are able to communicate with each other by using a system of different sounds.
3 Whales cannot swim under the water all the time because they need air to breathe.
4 (open answer)

⇨ Copymaster
Making a Gingerbread Whale

Children are given a recipe (an instructional text) and asked to sequence the instructions which have become muddled.

Making a Gingerbread Whale

Name _____ *Date* _____

Here is a recipe for making whales from gingerbread. The first section (What you need) is fine. The instructions in the second section (What you do) are all muddled up. Cut them out. Work out the order they should go in.

What you need:
- 3 teaspoons of golden syrup
- 250g self-raising flour
- 100g caster sugar
- a pinch of salt
- 3 teaspoons of ground ginger
- 50g margarine
- currants
- greased baking tray.

What you do:

Stir in the dry ingredients. Leave until the mixture is cool.

Press in the currant 'eyes'.

After 15 minutes the 'whales' should be cooked.

Sieve together the ginger, salt and flour.

Shape the mixture into 'whale' shapes.

Lay the 'whale' shapes onto the baking tray.

When the oven is up to heat, carefully place the baking tray in the oven.

Melt together the margarine, syrup and sugar.

Turn the oven on, to 335 degrees C (Gas Mark 3).

Focus on Comprehension Teacher's Book 'B'   Text © Louis Fidge 1999 Illustrations © Nelson 1999   Published by Thomas Nelson and Sons Ltd

FURTHER TEACHING OPPORTUNITIES

Text level

Reading comprehension

▶ Evaluate the advertisement for its impact, appeal and honesty. Focus on how information about the product is presented. Does it make any exaggerated claims? What tactics are used for grabbing attention? Does it use any linguistic devices such as alliteration? Ask children how successful they think it is.

Writing composition

▶ Use the advertisement as a model for designing a poster for a school event or an imaginary product.

Sentence level

Grammatical awareness

▶ Evaluate the use of adjectives in this and other advertisements. Try reading them and leaving out the adjectives to see what a difference it makes.

Sentence construction and punctuation

▶ Notice the use of exclamations, and the use of capital letters for emphasis and bullet points for clarity in the advertisement.

Word level

Spelling

▶ Brainstorm adjectives that end in the suffixes 'ful' (wonderful) and 'ive' (attractive) that might be used to persuade. Extend this to any other words ending in these suffixes and 'tion', 'ic', 'ist' for spelling activities.

Vocabulary extension

▶ Have fun making up alliterative sentences or phrases, such as great graphics, fantastic fun.

ANSWERS

Thinking back

1 The purpose of advertisements is to persuade people to buy things.
2 The advertisement is trying to sell a video game called Racing Rockets.
3 The advertisement says that the graphics are great.
4 The jingle used is: Find it! View it! Don't hang around. Get it and do it!
5 The advertisement is telling you to hurry because they are going fast.

Thinking about it

1 (open answer)
2 You can tell the game has just come out because the advertisement says it is new.
3 (open answer) Sensational means causing great excitement.
4 (open answer) Some of the claims made about the product are: it is sensational, it has great graphics, it offers fantastic fun and amazing action.
5 (open answer) Advertisers often use famous people to advertise their products, because ordinary people look up to them and are likely to be influenced by what they say.

Thinking it through

1 (open answer) All these devices are basically used to make certain things stand out.
2 (open answer) Advertisers tend to use short sentences. People need to be able to get the message and information quickly without having to put in too much effort.
3 (open answer)
4 (open answer)

➡ *Copymaster*
Advertising in the Local Paper
Several advertisements, typical of the adverts at the back of all local newspapers, are provided. Children are asked questions related to them.

Advertising in the Local Paper

Name _____ *Date* _____

1 FREE WOOD for logs or firewood, and posts. Richmond 487.

2 DESK for child. White. Good condition. £8. Richmond 576.

3 FISHING REEL. Good condition, with spool and line
cost new £40 sell £10. Richmond 578 (eves only).

4 TROUSERS BOYS' blue/grey as new £8. Richmond 575 (eves
only) 6–10.30 p.m.

5 TOY DOG pull-a-long puppy £3. Carousel £3. Radio £1.
Richmond 635.

6 CHILD'S BED RAIL £7. Baby sling £15. Trike £8. Richmond
676.

7 RECORD PLAYER £10. Plus record cabinet £9. Richmond 456
(eves and weekends) after 7 p.m.

8 STAINLESS STEEL sink unit. Double drainer with base and
taps £10. Richmond 504.

1 How much is the desk?_____   2 What colour is it? _____

3 How could you find out more about it? _____

4 Can you tell: a) how old it is?_____ b) what it is made from? _____

5 Do you think it is worth the money? Why? _____

6 Which telephone number would you ring for the toy dog? _____

7 What information is given about the sink? _____

8 Is number 4 a bargain? Why? _____

**Pretend this is your bike and you want to
sell it. Write a short advertisement for it
for your local newspaper.**

_____

_____

_____

Focus on Comprehension Teacher's Book 'B'   Text © Louis Fidge 1999   Illustrations © Nelson 1999   Published by Thomas Nelson and Sons Ltd

FURTHER TEACHING OPPORTUNITIES

Text level

Reading comprehension

▶ Focus on the fact that Elizabeth has just started a new school, having come from a different country. (How can we tell this by the way Elizabeth speaks?) Consider some of the problems she might face. What changes would be necessary? What does the passage itself tell us about Elizabeth? Ian? Miss Gregg?

Writing composition

▶ Ask children to write about times when they have felt lonely or isolated. Where were they? What had happened? What was the problem? How did it resolve itself?

▶ List the sorts of things that children could do to make a newcomer feel welcome in your classroom.

Sentence level

Grammatical awareness

▶ Use the passage as an opportunity for reviewing children's knowledge of word classes (parts of speech). Ask them to find the nouns, verbs, adjectives, adverbs or pronouns in the passage and discuss their functions. Leave them out and see what happens!

Sentence construction and punctuation

▶ Revise the conventions for punctuating speech in writing, by reference to the text.

Word level

Spelling

▶ Find the word 'laugh' in the text. Compare it with the word 'caught' and note the difference in pronunciation, even though they have the same letter pattern. Think of other words with common letter patterns but with different pronunciations, such as 'tough, through, though, trough; hour, journey, could, route, four'.

Vocabulary extension

▶ Look at the compound word 'doorway' and note how it is constructed. Brainstorm other compound words and write them on the board. Draw attention to those where the pronunciation does not always aid spelling such as 'cupboard'.

ANSWERS

Thinking back

1 Ian wanted to be Elizabeth's friend.
2 The children laughed at Ian because his eyes were different colours.
3 Elizabeth sat next to Ian Fuller in class.
4 When the bell went everybody ran outside.
5 Elizabeth followed Ian out to play.

Thinking about it

1 Ian didn't have any friends because the other children made fun of him.
2 (open answer)
3 Mrs Gregg was the teacher.
4 You can tell Mrs Gregg is surprised at Elizabeth by the way she says her name.
5 You can tell Mrs Gregg is a nice teacher by the way she didn't embarrass Elizabeth by asking her any more questions and by the way she smiled at her.

Thinking it through

1 The children laughed at Ian.
2 Elizabeth didn't mind Ian's eyes. The text says that she thought they were quite special.
3 (open answer)
4 (open answer)

⇨ *Copymaster* **A Friend in Need**

Elizabeth is in hospital. Ian takes her some presents. What should he take? Children are given some basic information about Elizabeth and a list of possible presents Ian chooses from. Based on the information they have, children have to make reasoned guesses.

A Friend in Need

Name _____   Date _____

Elizabeth is in hospital. Ian decided to take her five things to cheer her up. Read the information about Elizabeth.
What five things do you think Ian took her?

Elizabeth is nine tomorrow, but she will have to spend her birthday in hospital. She loves reading and music.
Elizabeth misses her friends and her garden (she helps her dad plant the vegetables and flowers). Elizabeth's favourite pastimes are drawing and doing jigsaw puzzles. She doesn't like sweets very much, or fruit juice. She is not very punctual and hates wearing a watch.

✓	Ian would take ...	Reason
	some reading books	
	some fruit juice	
	a board game	
	some felt tip pens	
	her watch	
	a birthday card	
	a CD of her favourite pop group	
	a photograph of her friends	
	a bunch of grapes	
	a box of chocolates	
	some flowers	
	a brush and comb	

Focus on Comprehension Teacher's Book 'B'   Text © Louis Fidge 1999 Illustrations © Nelson 1999   Published by Thomas Nelson and Sons Ltd

FURTHER TEACHING OPPORTUNITIES

Text level

Reading comprehension

▶ Read the passage and discuss some of the problems faced by Jackson. What sort of a person was he? What can we learn about him from the text? Ask the children to describe him in their own words, using whatever clues are available in the text, and their imagination.

▶ Examine and discuss some of the descriptive words and phrases used in the passage.

▶ Ask children to conjecture as to how Jackson became homeless.

▶ Find, read and compare some other books written by Leon Garfield.

Writing composition

▶ Consider and write down some of the problems faced by homeless people.

▶ Jackson and the dog strike up an unlikely friendship. Get children to write about some of the adventures they experience together.

Sentence level

Grammatical awareness

▶ There are some very powerful and descriptive verbs used in the story.

▶ Jackson does not always speak in standard English. Read the things he says and discuss the lack of agreement in some of the sentences.

Sentence construction and punctuation

▶ Read the passage again, noting particularly the use of commas, and the role they play in helping meaning.

Word level

Spelling

▶ Find the word 'terrible' in the text. Ask children to supply words ending in either 'able' or 'ible'. Classify them according to spelling, checking with a dictionary where there is uncertainty. Do the same with words ending in 'tion' and 'sion'.

Vocabulary extension

▶ Distinguish the two forms: it's (contracted it is) and its (possessive - no apostrophe). Encourage children to understand the distinction between the two. (Find an example of 'its' in the text.)

ANSWERS

Thinking back

The dog was nearly as big as a <u>donkey</u>. It had <u>eyes</u> like street lamps and <u>jaws</u> like an oven door. When somebody <u>threw</u> a bucket of water over it, the dog <u>snarled</u> with rage. Jackson <u>hid</u> his pie and <u>told</u> the dog to go away. <u>Jackson</u> said he was frozen and <u>hungry</u>. The dog would not go away, so Jackson gave it <u>some</u> (or <u>half</u>) of his pie.

Thinking about it

1 It was very cold. It was snowing.
2 It says that the dog had lean sides.
3 (open answer) Jackson did not want the dog coming near him.
4 (open answer) From the picture you can tell that Jackson is in a town, sheltering in a doorway.
5 (open answer) You can tell Jackson is poor by the way he is dressed.
6 (open answer) Jackson does not speak in grammatically correct sentences. For example he says, 'I'm froze and hungry!'

Thinking it through

1 (open answer)
2 (open answer) Some of the fierce words used are: glare, savage, snarled, growled, terrible, fearful.
3 (open answer) It probably means that as snow flakes landed on the dog's nose they melted.
4 (open answer) The dog 'talked' to Jackson with its eyes and its actions.
5 (open answer)

➡️ *Copymaster*   **The New Bike**
This copymaster requires children to sequence six pictures to tell part of a story. The story ends in a bit of a moral dilemma. Children have then to predict how it might continue.

➡ The New Bike

Name _____   Date _____

- ▶ Cut out the pictures and arrange them so they tell a story.
- ▶ In your book, write an ending for the story.
- ▶ What should the boy do?
- ▶ Should he stay and look for his bike or go home and face the music?
- ▶ What will happen?

Focus on Comprehension Teacher's Book 'B'   Text © Louis Fidge 1999 Illustrations © Nelson 1999   Published by Thomas Nelson and Sons Ltd

FURTHER TEACHING OPPORTUNITIES

Text level

Reading comprehension

▶ This unit contains four very different poems. Read and discuss each one separately. Decide what type of poem each one is; for example, is it a poem about a moral dilemma, an Acrostic poem, an alphabet poem or a riddle? Consider whether the poems do, or do not use rhyme. Introduce terms into the discussion, such as rhyme, alliteration, rhythm, rhyming couplets, stanza, and explain their meanings.

Writing composition

▶ Encourage children to write a poem in the style of one from the unit. Produce a finished poem through revision, such as by deleting, adding, or changing words, reorganising words or lines and by experimenting with language generally.

Sentence level

Grammatical awareness

▶ Use the poem about bullying to review work on pronouns. Identify the pronouns in the poem and decide whether they are singular or plural.

Sentence construction and punctuation

▶ Read the poems again, paying particular attention to the punctuation, and discussing how important it is, in reading aloud effectively.

Word level

Spelling

▶ Have a 'syllable search'. Ask children to find and list five one-, two-, and three-syllable words in the poems. Extend this by asking children to think of five four-syllable words, and to write them down, showing the syllable boundaries in each.

Vocabulary extension

▶ Find three compound words in the poems. How many compound words can be made, starting with the following: some, any, no?

ANSWERS

Thinking back
1 False.
2 True.
3 True.
4 False.
5 True.

Thinking about it
1 a) It was written on a Friday.
  b) Most of the events took place at school.
  c) (open answer)
2 The answer was a mirror.
3 (open answer)
4 (open answer) It probably means a thunderstorm.

Thinking it through
1 a) (open answer)
  b) (open answer)
2 (open answer)
3 (open answer)
4 (open answer)

▢▶ *Copymaster*
Thinking About Poetry
This proforma can be applied to most poems. It asks children to reflect on the content, structure and other features of any poem they have read.

⇨ Thinking About Poetry

Name _____ Date _____

Title of poem _____ Poet _____

What is the poem about? _____

_____

_____

_____

Is it a particular type of poem? (such as nonsense, shape poem)

_____

Does it have: a) verses? _____ b) a chorus? _____

Does it rhyme? _____

Is there anything special about the way the poet uses language

in the poem? _____

_____

Write some words or expressions you liked from the poem:

_____

_____

_____

What would you tell your friend about the poem?

_____

_____

Focus on Comprehension Teacher's Book 'B'   Text © Louis Fidge 1999 Illustrations © Nelson 1999   Published by Thomas Nelson and Sons Ltd

FURTHER TEACHING OPPORTUNITIES

Text level

Reading comprehension

▶ Explain to children that this is a piece of autobiographical writing that is true. What clues are there that Nebiyou comes from a different culture?

▶ After reading it discuss what sort of problems Nebiyou faced and the sort of life he led. How did children respond to his plight? How would Nebiyou have felt at different points in the story?

▶ In what sense could this be seen as a piece of persuasive writing? Look for examples of emotive language used: for example, 'Who cares anyway?'

Writing composition

▶ Present Nebiyou's story in an expanded form, fleshing out some of the sections: for example, the time he lived with his mother.

Sentence level

Grammatical awareness

▶ Take a section of the story and experiment by omitting particular classes of words: for instance, leave out all the nouns or verbs. Discuss how this helps focus on the grammatical functions of these words.

Sentence construction and punctuation

▶ Take some of the sentences from the text, rewrite them, jumbling up the word order. Ask children to rewrite them, without reference to the text for comparison.

Word level

Spelling

▶ Find the word 'direction' in the passage. Identify the root word. Note that a verb is changed to a noun by the addition of the suffix '-tion'. Change these verbs to nouns by adding 'tion'. a) protect, act, correct; b) generate, educate, decorate; c) organise, prepare, explore. Consider what changes are required to do this.

Vocabulary extension

▶ Research the names of places: for example, an orphanage is a place for orphans. Look up the following in a dictionary: a monastery, a nunnery, a university.

ANSWERS

Thinking back

Nebiyou lived with his mother when he was small. When his mother died, he went to live with his father.
Nebiyou's father went to fight but did not return.
Some soldiers took Nebiyou to Kenya in a big car.
Nebiyou was sent to a refugee camp called Kakuma.

Thinking about it

1 (open answer)

2 You know that Nebiyou's parents did not live together because it says that Nebiyou lived with his mother when he was small and went to live with his father when his mother died.

3 Nebiyou's father was a soldier.

4 You can tell there was a war because it says that Nebiyou's father was a soldier and that he went to a 'fighting place'.

5 (open answer)

6 (open answer)

Thinking it through

1 (open answer)

2 You can tell there was panic at the time because Nebiyou says that everything was messy, cars were driving everywhere and people were afraid of one another.

3 a) An orphan is someone whose mother and father have died.
b) An orphanage is a home where orphans can live.
c) A refugee is someone who has been forced to leave their own country.

4 (open answer)

➡ *Copymaster* **I Don't Care**

This story is from India and has a moral. It is in the form of a cloze procedure for children to complete.

 # I Don't Care

Name _____ Date _____

Read this story. Think of a sensible word to go in each gap.

The only thing Anwar could think of was water. He was _____

very hot! The road was _____ and dusty. Then he saw

another well. 'I expect it _____ be dry, like the _____,'

he said to himself. As he got _____ he saw a _____

dog lying beside it. Anwar could see its _____ it was so thin.

'I don't care about _____. I just need water. Get out of my

_____,' Anwar said. He was desperate to get to the

_____. He picked up a _____ and dropped it into the

well. For a second _____ was silence and then Plop!

'_____!' cried Anwar. The dog _____ pitifully.

There was _____ bucket or rope _____ Anwar had to

climb down the inside the well. He had to _____ on by his

fingers and toes. At _____ he reached the _____. He

poured some cool water over _____ head and drank great

gulps of it until he felt completely _____.

Suddenly a picture of the _____ old dog came into his

_____. 'He is just as much in _____ of a drink as I was,'

he thought. Then _____ idea came into his head.

When he reached the top of the well the _____ looked up.

Anwar smiled. 'Here you are,' he said and _____ out his boot –

_____ of water!

Focus on Comprehension Teacher's Book 'B' Text © Louis Fidge 1999 Illustrations © Nelson 1999 Published by Thomas Nelson and Sons Ltd

FURTHER TEACHING OPPORTUNITIES

Text level

Reading comprehension
▶ Discuss how information is presented, by use of pictures and text. There is a saying that 'a picture saves a thousand words'. Discuss what this might mean.

Writing composition
▶ Ask children to write a day's diary entry about their routine and life in the camp, based on the evidence from the unit.
▶ Ask children to comment on major differences between their lifestyle and those of the orphans. Encourage them to think of some of the good points such as the camaraderie and the outdoor life, and some of the disadvantages (no parents, limited diet).

Sentence level

Grammatical awareness
▶ Look for words in the captions that have suffixes: for example, turns, making, given. Decide what the root word of each is, and what type of word it is, such as a noun or verb.

Sentence construction and punctuation
▶ Notice the use of the dash in 'Washing – a job everyone hates!' Explain that a dash in cases like this, serves a similar function to a comma, signalling the need to pause, and separating one part of a sentence from another.

Word level

Spelling
▶ Have a 'small word hunt' looking for smaller words hiding inside longer words, such as 'water'.

Vocabulary extension
▶ Search for a number of words from the captions beginning with the same letter. Sort these words into alphabetical order.

ANSWERS

Thinking back
1 False.
2 True.
3 False.
4 False.
5 True.
6 False.

Thinking about it
1 The weather is usually hot and dry. You can tell from the pictures.
2 (open answer)
3 (open answer)
4 (open answer)
5 (open answer)

Thinking it through
1 (open answer)
2 (open answer)
3 (open answer)
4 (open answer)

⇨▶ *Copymaster*
Every Picture Tells a Story
Much of the information in the unit is in the form of pictures and captions. Children are asked to study a picture of an accident very carefully, describe what they can see, and to pose questions that they would like to have answered.

Every Picture Tells a Story

Name _____   Date _____

There has been an accident.

Look carefully at the picture and describe what you can see.

_____

_____

_____

_____

_____

_____

_____

There are also many things you cannot tell from the picture. On the other side of this sheet, write five questions about things you would like to know more about.

Focus on Comprehension Teacher's Book 'B'   Text © Louis Fidge 1999 Illustrations © Nelson 1999   Published by Thomas Nelson and Sons Ltd

FURTHER TEACHING OPPORTUNITIES

Text level

Reading comprehension

▶ What can be learnt about the characters of Sanjay, Neetu and Grandpa Chatterji from the text?

▶ What can be learnt about Sanjay and Neetu's home?

▶ What clues are there that Grandpa Chatterji comes from a different culture?

▶ Explain how the children might have felt at various points throughout the passage.

▶ How does the author manage to build up tension and excitement in the story?

▶ Find, read and compare different stories by Jamila Gavin.

Writing composition

▶ Ask the children to imagine that a very important visitor came to the school and that they were picked to show the visitor around. How would they feel? What would they wear? How would they behave?

Sentence level

Grammatical awareness

▶ Reread the description of Grandpa Chatterji, drawing special attention to the use of adjectives.

Sentence construction and punctuation

▶ Note the use of hyphens when pulling together two words like 'dark-brown, long-toed'. Look for other examples in reading books and try to decide how and when hyphens are used.

Word level

Spelling

▶ Use the text to find examples of the soft 'g' sound, such as 'emerged', 'gently' and the hard 'g' sound, such as 'go', 'Grandpa'. Ask children to suggest other words for both sets.

Vocabulary extension

▶ Explore and discuss the implications of words which imply gender, such as grandfather, grandmother. Brainstorm and come up with as many gender-related words as possible, related to people.

ANSWERS

Thinking back

1 True.

2 True.

3 False.

4 False.

5 True.

6 False.

Thinking about it

1 The children were nervous because they had never seen Grandpa Chatterji before.

2 They probably hid behind the sofa because they were embarrassed and nervous.

3 You can tell he had come on a long journey because the children's parents had been to meet him and he had brought luggage with him.

4 (open answer) He might have taken his shoes off, or he might have not been used to wearing shoes.

5 It says his face was wrinkly.

6 (open answer) He was probably friendly because his face is described as 'kind'.

Thinking it through

1 (open answer) The children were probably shy because they had not seen Grandpa Chatterji before.

2 (open answer)

3 (open answer)

4 (open answer)

▶ *Copymaster*   **Fact or Opinion?**

An important skill in reading is to be able to differentiate between facts and opinions. The copymaster encourages children to do this.

 # Fact or Opinion?

Name _____ Date _____

 **Shagufta wrote some things about Luton. After each statement, write if it is a fact or an opinion.**

Luton is in the county of Bedfordshire. _____

I think the people in Luton are very friendly. _____

The town is about 40 kilometres north of London. _____

Luton has an airport. _____

Luton is the best place in the country to live in. _____

Luton Football team are great! _____

The library is in the centre of Luton. _____

I reckon the University of Luton is the best in England. _____

Write four facts about your school:

_____

_____

_____

Give your opinions:

Which is your favourite lesson?_____

Which pop group is best? _____

What sort of crisps are best? _____

What do you think the speed limit should be?_____

Which soap do you think is best on TV? _____